OECD Companion to the Inventory of Support Measures for Fossil Fuels 2021

OECD

BETTER POLICIES FOR BETTER LIVES

This document, as well as any data and map included herein, are without prejudice to the status of or sovereignty over any territory, to the delimitation of international frontiers and boundaries and to the name of any territory, city or area.

The statistical data for Israel are supplied by and under the responsibility of the relevant Israeli authorities. The use of such data by the OECD is without prejudice to the status of the Golan Heights, East Jerusalem and Israeli settlements in the West Bank under the terms of international law.

Note by Turkey
The information in this document with reference to "Cyprus" relates to the southern part of the Island. There is no single authority representing both Turkish and Greek Cypriot people on the Island. Turkey recognises the Turkish Republic of Northern Cyprus (TRNC). Until a lasting and equitable solution is found within the context of the United Nations, Turkey shall preserve its position concerning the "Cyprus issue".

Note by all the European Union Member States of the OECD and the European Union
The Republic of Cyprus is recognised by all members of the United Nations with the exception of Turkey. The information in this document relates to the area under the effective control of the Government of the Republic of Cyprus.

Please cite this publication as:
OECD (2021), *OECD Companion to the Inventory of Support Measures for Fossil Fuels 2021*, OECD Publishing, Paris, *https://doi.org/10.1787/e670c620-en*.

ISBN 978-92-64-42643-6 (print)
ISBN 978-92-64-96239-2 (pdf)

Foreword

As governments design measures to stimulate economies decimated by the COVID-19 crisis, they have a major opportunity to pursue a sustainable, inclusive recovery aligned with long-term goals to reduce greenhouse gas emissions. As well as investing in low-carbon energy, that means reviewing fossil-fuel subsidies, which not only encourage wasteful consumption but also often serve poorly their purported social goals of increasing energy access and affordability. Historically low energy prices resulting from the slump in economic activity provide a welcome chance to reform energy pricing, including fossil-fuel support.

There is little evidence, however, that governments are using COVID-19 recovery efforts and current market conditions as a spur for fossil-fuel subsidy reform. Many countries are funneling the bulk of stimulus funding to support fossil-fuel and related industries, often with no climate change or pollution reduction requirements attached. Without further conditions on support or focus on "green" recovery measures, we will miss the opportunity to "build back better". Support for fossil-fuel producers was already rising in 2019, with the latest OECD Inventory of Support Measures for Fossil Fuels registering a 30% increase in direct and indirect support for the production of fossil fuels, primarily in OECD countries. This increase drove a rise in total support to USD 178 billion.

Backsliding on support for fossil fuels demonstrates a concerning disconnect with the increasingly pressing climate emergency. It also underscores the need for ongoing efforts to enhance transparency on the many ways that governments continue to encourage fossil-fuel production and use. Supporting economies and societies through the COVID-19 crisis has to be a priority. But it need not entail a strengthening of support for polluting technologies.

The OECD Inventory identifies, measure by measure, the ways in which 50 OECD, G20 and European Union Eastern Partnership economies provide direct budgetary support or tax expenditures in favour of fossil fuels, documenting over 1 300 policies. In this way, the OECD provides a platform to help governments evaluate how scarce budgetary resources are prioritised and allocated – particularly relevant as the COVID-19-induced recession increases pressure on government budgets – and the coherence of spending with broader environmental and well-being goals. When combined OECD-IEA estimates are taken into account, fossil-fuel support adds up to USD 468 billion across 81 economies representing 90% of global total primary energy supply.

Fortunately, there is continued momentum to enhance transparency of support for fossil-fuel subsidies in other international fora, which is crucial for spreading best practices and sound policy-making. G20 economies continue to demonstrate leadership by stepping up to undertake peer reviews of support for fossil fuels – traditionally chaired by the OECD – with Argentina, Canada, France and India in the pipeline. New Zealand is seeking to reinvigorate momentum in the APEC fossil-fuel support reform agenda during its 2021 host year. Country reporting on fossil-fuel subsidies in the context of the UN Sustainable Development Goals indicator framework is due to start imminently. Direct reporting by countries will encourage the development of national inventories of subsidies and enhance awareness within and among countries of both the magnitude and nature of support.

Building on this momentum, this report proposes a novel methodology for a robust sequential approach to designing fossil-fuel subsidy reforms in OECD and G20 economies, to accelerate and enable greater traction in reform. The OECD stands ready to further support countries in reform, to help ensure sustainable consumption and production, boost resilience to future economic shocks and build more environmentally sustainable economies.

Acknowledgements

The preparation of this report was led by Justine Garrett of the Environment Directorate of the OECD under the supervision of Nathalie Girouard, Head of the Environmental Performance and Indicators Division, with drafting, statistical and analytical inputs and support from colleagues Mark Mateo, Sarah Miet and Amy Cano Prentice. Special thanks to colleagues Katjusha Boffa, Sophie Boissonade, Elizabeth Del Bourgo, Catherine Bremer, Enrico Conti, Natasha Cline-Thomas, Marie-Aurélie Elkurd, Marielle Guillaud, Jeremy Kundtz, Anita Lari, Flora Monsaingeon-Lavuri, Jacqueline Maher, Shellie Phillips, Pascale Rossignol, and Fiona Smyth for their excellent assistance and support in disseminating, communicating and finalising preparation of the publication, and to Andrew Johnston for his work editing the report.

Chapter 2 is adapted from a 2020 Environment Working Paper written by Assia Elgouacem, who also provided helpful comments and suggestions on the rest of the report. Grateful thanks to the several other OECD colleagues who provided comments: Helen Blake, Nils Axel Braathen, Carla Bertuzzi, Ivana Capozza, Miguel Cárdenas Rodríguez, Raffaella Centurelli, Kurt van Dender, Ivan Haščič, Guillaume Lecaros de Cossio, Alexander Mackie, Mauro Migotto, Evdokia Moïsé, Nelly Petkova, Alexa Piccolo, Jonas Teusch and Frédérique Zegel. Mark Mateo led expansion and update of the database (the Inventory). Deepika Sehdev contributed on the sectoral and ocean tagging data work and the drafting of the country notes document. Those who helped collect and update information for specific countries include: Cristian Cuta (Chile), Ellaine de Guzman (Finland, Iceland, Ireland, New Zealand and Norway), István Harkai (Hungary), the International Institute for Sustainable Development (Canada, India, Indonesia, Mexico, South Africa, United Kingdom), Silja Kralik (Estonia and Germany), Marija Linartaite (Latvia, Lithuania, Poland and Sweden), Maria Victoria Lottici (Argentina), Evgenia Mikhalkova (the Russian Federation), Caroline Nogueira (Brazil and Portugal), the OECD Green Action Task Force (EU Eastern Partnership countries), Bengisu Özenç (Turkey), Michael Polemis (Greece), and Gary Xie (People's Republic of China). The contributions of Éric Espinasse, Karine Lepron, Nobuko Miyachiyo, Samuel Pinto Ribeiro in developing the online database are gratefully acknowledged.

This report and the associated database were examined by the OECD Joint Meetings of Tax and Environment Experts and Joint Working Party on Trade and Environment; Working Party on Environmental Information delegates were also given the opportunity to comment. The report and database were also examined and approved for publication by the Committee on Fiscal Affairs, the Environment Policy Committee and the Trade Committee. Invaluable information, comments and other input concerning the report and the associated database were provided by these delegates and their colleagues in national and sub-national government administrations.

Executive summary

Rising support in OECD countries reverses five-year downward trend in fossil fuel subsidies

Reforming fossil-fuel subsidies is crucial to reducing greenhouse gas emissions and hence meeting climate change goals. Since 2009, G20 leaders have regularly affirmed their joint commitment to rationalise and phase out "inefficient fossil-fuel subsidies that encourage wasteful consumption" over the medium term, while ensuring targeted support for the poorest. The 2020 OECD Inventory of Support Measures for Fossil Fuels documents over 1 300 government budgetary transfers and tax expenditures that support the production and consumption of fossil fuels. This Companion draws on the Inventory's findings to provide insights on progress in reform.

The 2020 Inventory records fossil-fuel support in 50 OECD, G20 and European Union Eastern Partnership economies. Total support rose by 5% year-on-year to USD 178 billion in 2019, reversing a five-year downward trend. The increase was driven by a 30% rise in direct and indirect support for the production of fossil fuels, primarily in OECD countries, as governments provided additional funding and preferential tax treatment to help alleviate corporate debt and encourage fossil-fuel infrastructure investment. The massive upheaval to the global energy system caused by the COVID-19 crisis – both in terms of fuel prices and consumption – is set to enhance this trend, with many countries using COVID-19 recovery aid to shore up fossil-fuel and related industries.

But consumer support is declining, driven by the drop in fuel prices

Conversely, the crisis is enhancing 2019 reductions in support for fossil-fuel consumption due principally to the mechanical effect on consumption subsidies of the drop in average fuel prices, as governments continue to spend less subsidising energy costs for end users. The OECD-IEA combined estimates of government support for fossil fuels in 81 economies, which include fossil-fuel support provided through induced transfers (i.e. price regulation), fell by 19% year-on-year in 2019, to USD 468 billion. Support for consumption represented 89% of the overall figure. Policy changes played a limited role in the reduced estimates, with few positive reforms announced in the period. Similarly, government focus on providing immediate support to economies, firms and households in response to the COVID-19 pandemic does not appear to have translated into widespread, additional momentum to use low fuel prices to carry our pricing reform. Many governments have ignored or made only partial use of the major opportunity to prioritise sustainable investments and broader well-being objectives as they design and implement stimulus measures for economies battered by the COVID-19 crisis. Governments need to place further conditions on support and focus on "green" recovery measures to reorient their economies in the right direction.

Peer reviews generate lessons for fossil-fuel reform

Indonesia and Italy completed peer reviews of fossil-fuel support under the auspices of the G20 in 2019, chaired by the OECD. Reviews for Argentina and Canada are under way, and France and India committed in August 2019 to follow suit as the next review pair. Defining what constitutes an "inefficient fossil-fuel subsidy that encourages wasteful consumption" for the purposes of the overarching G20 commitment remains a challenge, but the growing body of peer reviews is helping to draw out differences in interpretation, providing an important first step towards a possible future common definition. Peer reviews are also providing insight into how countries might go about the reform process, and the potential vulnerability of reform to the prevailing political environment – underscoring the need for ongoing efforts to improve transparency of support and continued monitoring by the G20 and other organisations. Examples of good practice include efforts to reform the solid fossil-fuel industry in Germany, "pro-poor" reform efforts in Indonesia through better targeting of electricity subsidies, Italy's use of model-based macroeconomic assessment to assess the possible impact of phase-out of support measures on economic activity, and fuel pricing and taxation reform in Mexico.

Tracking fossil-fuel support in the context of the UN Sustainable Development Goals

Country reporting against SDG indicator 12.c.1, "Amount of fossil-fuel subsidies per unit of GDP (production and consumption)", is due to commence soon. UN Environment's methodology to help guide country reporting and underpin national and global measurement of support – developed with the OECD and the International Institute of Sustainable Development – invites countries to report disaggregated information on individual support measures, adopting the Inventory approach. Countries are to report on direct transfers, induced transfers, and – as an optional sub-indicator for countries that do not yet have the information or resources available – tax expenditures, other revenue forgone and under-pricing of goods and services. Particularly for OECD countries, which deliver most (or all) support to fossil fuels through tax expenditures, tax expenditure data is intrinsic to establishing an accurate picture of progress towards the SDG indicator. The same can be said for at least the partner economies included in the Inventory, in which 43% of the total value of support is provided by tax expenditures.

Enhancing the interpretation of tax expenditure data

The OECD is considering how the interpretation of tax expenditure data might be enriched, prompted by ongoing exchanges with member countries on their measurement and comparability. Using an external rather than domestic benchmark – such as an internationally agreed reference carbon price – is one option, although the resulting calculation of revenue reveals less about countries' domestic contexts. Ireland and Sweden are considering how effective carbon price analysis might complement national tax reference rates, together with an expert sub-group of the London group on environmental accounts. Two further avenues for research are growth decomposition analysis, to help assess whether changes in support arise from explicit reform or simply structural changes to the underlying domestic benchmark tax regime; and effective tax rate analysis for production of fossil fuels (i.e. corporate effective rates), to show the extent to which tax expenditures provide investment incentives in upstream fossil-fuel industry segments.

Methodology for a sequential approach in designing fossil-fuel subsidy reforms

The trends highlighted in this report illuminate the challenges that governments face in gaining traction for reform. To help spur enduring change, this report offers a sequential framework to assist OECD and G20 governments assess and address the effects of fossil-fuel support measures and their reform. Each step can be tailored to fit countries' contexts and underpin individual reform processes. The framework proposes several analytical tools to facilitate each step, from identifying the most distorting government support measures, to crafting alternative or complementary policies to mitigate any adverse impacts of reform. Including a full suite of assessments in designing reform measures should minimise the risk of political backlash and backsliding that too often accompanies reform. Being modular by construction, the sequential approach also enables different steps to be undertaken in isolation as countries identify specific needs, and as capacity to conduct analysis becomes available. Enhancing transparency on the ways governments deliver support to fossil-fuel users and producers remains an essential first step towards reform, underscoring the ongoing relevance of the Inventory's primary mission to provide comprehensive information on policies that support fossil fuels and shed light on how public resources are used.

Table of contents

Tables

Figures

Boxes

Acronyms and abbreviations

APEC	Asia-Pacific Economic Cooperation
BUEGO	Bottom-up economic and geological oil field production model
CARES	Coronavirus Aid, Relief and Economic Security Act
CEQ	Commitment to Equity Institute
CFE	Comisión Federal de Electricidad, or Federal Electricity Commission
CGE	Computable general-equilibrium model
CHP	Combined heat and power
CIT	Corporate income tax
CNG	Compressed natural gas
CO$_2$	Carbon dioxide
COVID-19	Coronavirus disease of 2019
CSE	Consumer support estimate
EATR	Effective average tax rate
ECR	Effective carbon rates
EMTR	Effective marginal tax rate
ETR	Effective tax rate
ETS	Emissions trading system
EaP	European Union Eastern Partnership
EU-ETS	European Union Emissions Trading System
FARI	Fiscal Analysis of Resource Industries
FFS	Fossil-fuel support
G7	Group of Seven
G20	Group of Twenty
GDP	Gross domestic product
GHG	Greenhouse gas
GSI	Global Subsidies Initiative
GSSE	General services support estimate

IAEG	Inter-Agency and Expert Group
IBOs	Interdepartementale Beleidsonderzoeken, or Interdepartmental Policy Reviews
IEA	International Energy Agency
IEPS	Impuesto Especial sobre Producción y Servicios por Enajenación de Gasolina y Diesel, or Special Tax on Production and Services for the Alienation of Petrol and Diesel
IISD	International Institute for Sustainable Development
IMF	International Monetary Fund
LNG	Liquid natural gas
LPG	Liquid petroleum gas
METRO	ModElling Trade at the OECD
ODA	Overseas development assistance
PCGB	Paris Collaborative on Green Budgeting
PEMEX	Petróleos Mexicanos, or Mexican Petroleum
PSE	Producer support estimate
PSO	Public service obligation
RRT	Resource rent tax
SDG	Sustainable Development Goal
SME	Small and medium-sized enterprise
SOE	State-owned enterprise
TEU	OECD Taxing Energy Use
TSE	Total support estimate
UN	United Nations
UPD	United Poverty Database
USD	United States dollars
VAT	Value-added tax

1 Tracking progress in reforming support for fossil fuels

Chapter 1 draws on data compiled for the 2020 edition of the OECD Inventory to describe broad trends in the magnitude and nature of fossil-fuel subsidies in 50 OECD, G20 and European Union Eastern Partnership (EaP) economies, and how these relate to recent policy changes and reforms in-country. The chapter discusses the implications of the COVID-19 crisis, and resulting oil price crash, for reform. It includes sectoral breakdown of support measures, as well as an assessment of support measures in EaP countries and measures related to ocean sustainability, as part of ongoing efforts to enhance transparency of government support. Section 1.2 discusses efforts to track and reform fossil fuel subsidies in multilateral fora, including in the context of the G20's framework for voluntary, reciprocal peer reviews and the Sustainable Development Goal fossil-fuel subsidy indicator 12.c.1. It looks at recent efforts to enhance the interpretation of tax expenditure data given the prevalence of tax expenditures in the measures documented by the Inventory.

1.1. Rising support for fossil-fuel production reverses five-year downward trend

1.1.1. Support for fossil-fuel production rose 30% in 2019

The OECD Inventory of Support Measures for Fossil Fuels records government spending that provides a benefit or preference for the production or consumption of fossil fuels over alternatives. The latest edition of the Inventory documents more than 1 300 budgetary transfers and tax expenditures in 50 countries (OECD, 2020[1]).[1] The Inventory countries include the OECD member countries,[2] Argentina, Brazil, the People's Republic of China (hereafter "China"), India, Indonesia, the Russian Federation, South Africa and the European Union (EU) Eastern Partnership (EaP) countries: Armenia, Azerbaijan, Belarus, Georgia, Republic of Moldova and Ukraine. Total fossil-fuel support across these 50 countries rose by 5% year-on-year to USD 178 billion in 2019, reversing a five-year downward trend (OECD, 2018[2]), (OECD, 2015[3]).

This increase was driven by a 30% rise in direct and indirect support for fossil fuel production, primarily in OECD member countries (Figure 1.1, Figure 1.3). In 2019, oil and gas sectors in several countries received additional assistance. Most of this was direct budgetary support to alleviate corporate debt and help finance fossil-fuel infrastructure investments, as well as tax provisions providing preferential treatment for capital expenditures for fossil-fuel production. Producer support estimates (PSE) across Inventory countries increased by 9% compared with 2017 levels. General services support estimates (GSSE), which the Inventory methodology attributes in majority share to production, doubled.[3] Together, these estimates amounted to USD 53 billion in 2019, sufficient to drive the overall increase documented by the Inventory – even though 70% of support measures continue to go to fossil-fuel consumption (Figure 1.1).[4] Total OECD country support for fossil fuels rose by 9% from 2017 levels in 2019, to reach USD 105 billion. The increase deepens the cleavage in overall support figures between OECD member countries and the 13 non-OECD G20 and EaP partner economies included in the Inventory, in which support levels hovered at around USD 75 billion per year between 2017 and 2019 (Figure 1.1).

Figure 1.1. Rising OECD country fossil fuel production support drives increase in total support levels

Total support in OECD member countries (left) and selected non-OECD G20 and EaP economies (right) by year and type of support

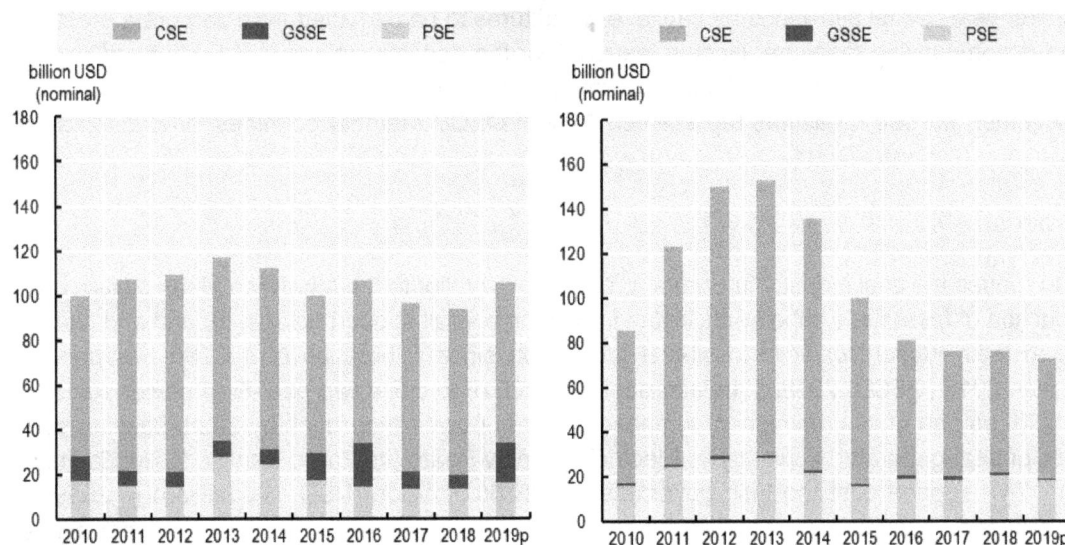

Note: CSE = consumer support estimates. GSSE = general services support estimates. PSE = producer support estimates. The OECD Inventory Methodology attributes GSSE support as benefiting producers at a 3:1 ratio when compared with consumers, so increases in both PSE and GSSE are relevant. Figure 1.1 sets out the arithmetic sum of the individual support measures identified in the Inventory. . Because they focus on budgetary costs and revenue forgone, the estimates for G20 and EaP economies do not reflect the totality of support provided by way of fuel price control measures (see Figure 1.3).
Source: (OECD, 2020[1]).

North American countries were responsible for 51% of the hike in OECD member country production support measures. Mexico's fossil-fuel support more than tripled between 2017 and 2019 after the administration that assumed office in December 2018 sought to shore up Pemex, the heavily indebted, majority state-owned petroleum company. The administration's assistance has included direct transfers to absorb Pemex debt and pension liabilities, and to support infrastructure such as a new oil refinery in the state of Tabasco, as well as steps to enhance tax deductions for Pemex's shared profit rights (Webber, 2019[4]). Mexico's measures are the main source of the USD 6 billion increase in total Inventory figures from 2017 to 2019. They raise Mexico's proportion of total Inventory support levels to 10%, and its share of OECD member country support to 16%. They contrast with significant progress in previous years through energy price liberalisation reform, aimed at eliminating support for gasoline and diesel fuel consumption provided through the country's floating excise tax (*IEPS, or Impuesto Especial sobre Producción y Servicios por Enajenación de Gasolina y Diesel*) (OECD, 2018[2]), (OECD, 2015[3]).

The United States increased its total support for fossil fuels by 28% between 2017 and 2019, principally through pre-existing measures enhancing federal support for oil and gas exploration and development. The country now represents 5% of total Inventory support levels, although US support as a share of GDP remains among the lowest in the Inventory. Three measures contributed strongly to the increase. A 1990 tax credit amounting to 15% of investment costs related to enhanced oil recovery is triggered when the reference price of oil fell below a specified level. A 1986 mechanism enables tax deduction of certain exploration and development costs associated with successful domestic oil and gas well investments. And a measure introduced in 1926 allows producers to claim a fixed percentage of revenue as a depletion allowance (i.e. rather than deduction of capital expenses in step with the depletion of resources over time), to help recover capitalised costs at an accelerated rate. These measures show how steps taken in different economic, political and environmental contexts – and which may or may not be suited to current circumstances – can continue to have a material impact several decades on.

Beyond North America, production support measures also rose significantly in the United Kingdom, by 37% between 2017 and 2019. This increase was principally due to the operation of two existing measures. "Ring-fence" corporate income tax relief for oil and gas extraction activities in the North Sea, which enables a 100% first-year capital allowance for capital expenditures to be deducted from corporate profits, rose by 22%. An accompanying measure, income tax relief for the decommissioning of fields by allowing capital expenditures to be deducted in full from corporate profits in the year in which they are incurred, rose by 55%. Together, the two measures represented 11% of OECD member countries' production support for 2019.

European efforts to scale back the solid fossil-fuel industry continue

Efforts to reduce the coal industry in Europe provide some relief to the otherwise bleak picture on support for production of fossil fuels, albeit with limited impact on overall support figures. Ireland and Norway have decreased their support for solid fossil-fuel production since publication of the last Companion to the Inventory in 2018 (OECD, 2018[2]). Ireland decided in 2019 to close two peat-fired power stations by the end of 2020 as part of its commitment to phase out peat power generation by 2028, ceasing support for purchase of peat-generated power by its Electricity Supply Board (its Public Service Obligation levy) (Lee, 2019[5]).[5] This support cost the Irish government EUR 65.5 million (USD 73.3 million) in 2019, a figure already reduced from previous years. At the end of 2017, Norway ceased providing an operating subsidy to prop up its flailing state-owned Store Norske coal-mining company operating in the Arctic territory of Svalbard, with no support registered under this measure in the Inventory from 2018 on (although support for decommissioning was set to continue through 2020).[6] NOK 144 million (USD 17 million) was spent on this measure in 2017.

Building on its successful phase-out of budgetary support for domestic hard-coal production in North Rhine-Westphalia in 2018, Germany closed its last black coal mine in December 2018, and plans to phase out its already diminishing lignite production (The Associated Press, 2018[6]), (Steenblik and Mateo, 2020[7]). Spain achieved its target of closing all of its coal mines by the end of 2018 and shut down more than half of its coal-fired power plants in mid-2020, with these operations said to be unprofitable (CGTN, 2020[8]).[7]

Most Western European countries are now members of the Powering Past Coal Alliance, which commits them to phase out by 2030 coal power that is unabated, i.e. without carbon capture and storage (PPCA, 2021[9]). Western Europe's retreat from coal and shift to cleaner sources of electricity generation has helped reduce the share of coal in the electricity mix of OECD member countries (Figure 1.2). Coal's share of gross OECD electricity production fell from 34% in 2010 to 22% in 2019, while the share for renewables rose from 18% to 28% and the share for natural gas from 24% to 30%. These shifts reflect decreasing levels of support for coal in OECD member countries, as coal-fired power plant closures have reduced both producer and consumer support, including due to reduced coal demand (Figure 1.2). Support for coal in OECD member countries – which nevertheless continue to provide the bulk of support to coal as documented by the Inventory (76%) – fell to USD 9 billion in 2019, from over USD 16 billion in 2010.

Figure 1.2. The shift away from coal-fired electricity generation in OECD member countries reflects a fall in coal support levels

Total support estimate for coal (bar chart) and % share of electricity generation from coal (line chart) in OECD member countries

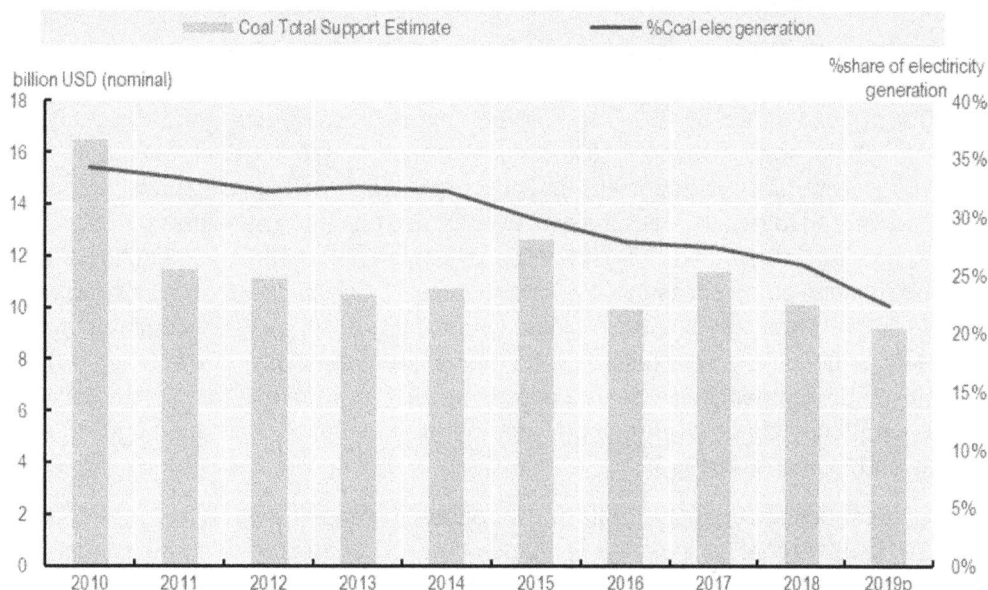

Source: Aggregations from (OECD, 2020[1]) and (IEA, 2020[10])

1.1.2. Inventory shows stable support for fossil-fuel use, but combined OECD-IEA numbers show a significant decline

Support estimates for the consumption of fossil fuels documented in the Inventory hovered between USD 125 billion and USD 131 billion annually from 2017 to 2019 (Figure 1.1). This stability was maintained despite fluctuations in average fuel prices, especially for oil, and despite the fact that that crude oil and petroleum products continue to attract the bulk of government support both in OECD and partner economies: 75% of the consumer support estimate, compared with 11% for natural gas, 10% for electricity and 4% for coal.[8] Inventory countries tend to support fossil-fuel consumption in ways other than under-pricing fuels – such as through preferential tax treatments of select fuels or usage – blunting the impact of international oil price fluctuations on Inventory estimates (see Section 1.2.3). The effects of oil price shifts are more evident when support is broken down between OECD member countries and the partner economies covered in the Inventory (Figure 1.1).

The picture of consumption support changes considerably when combined OECD-International Energy Agency (IEA) data are taken into account. The OECD and the IEA have been producing an annual joint estimate of support for fossil fuels since 2018, to facilitate a fuller assessment than that enabled by either the Inventory's cataloguing of budgetary and tax expenditure measures or the IEA's "price gap" approach.[9] The IEA derives its estimates of consumption subsidies by comparing observed, in-country energy prices with international reference prices (import- or export-parity). As a result, IEA estimates (and hence combined OECD-IEA figures) are closely tied to global oil price fluctuations.

The OECD-IEA combined estimates of government support for fossil fuels across 81 economies fell by 19% year-on-year in 2019, to USD 468 billion, with support for consumption representing 89% of the overall figure (Figure 1.3). Support fell principally because of the mechanical effect of the drop in average fuel prices on consumption subsidies, as governments spent less subsidising energy costs for end users. The 2019 estimates reverse a three-year upward trend in support numbers. Between 2016 and 2018, mounting oil prices prompted some countries to fully or partially reinstate, maintain or strengthen fossil-fuel price controls, and in other countries hampered energy price liberalisation and taxation reform efforts (OECD/IEA, 2019[11]). Policy changes played a limited role in the reduced estimates of consumption support in 2019, with few reforms announced.

China's consumer support estimates in the Inventory declined by 10%, driven by reductions in support for fuel use in domestic fishing after the government announced in 2015 that it intended to reduce these subsidies to 40% of 2014 levels by 2019, to help prevent overfishing and enhance industry efficiency (Zizhu, 2021[12]).[10] China now represents 13% of total consumer support documented in the Inventory. Support also fell in Egypt, Iran, Kazakhstan, Libya, Ukraine and Zimbabwe (Gould, Adam and Walton, 2020[13]). Egypt committed to reduce fuel subsidies by 40% and electricity subsidies by 75% in the 2019-20 financial year; it had eliminated electricity subsidies by the second half of 2019 (Middle East Monitor, 2019[14]). Iran raised petrol pump prices by 50% in November 2019, with drivers then paying twice as much per litre after the first 60 litres they buy each month (France 24, 2019[15]). Kazakhstan approved new cap rates for electricity, although the new rates still fall below the market cost of electricity production (IEA, 2020[16]). The Libyan government implemented price increases on kerosene for industrial and commercial end users to reach production cost, including to combat rampant international smuggling of subsidised kerosene (Lewis and Elumami, 2019[17]).

Conversely, countries such as Argentina, India and Indonesia increased support for fossil-fuel consumption in the period 2018-19. Argentina imposed a 90-day fuel price freeze in the retail fuel market from September 2019, with accompanying producer support, after the Argentine peso plunged in August 2019 (Duranona et al., 2019[18]). As a result of the COVID-19 pandemic, the price freeze was extended into 2020, with a slight price increase enabled in December 2019 (Diamante, 2020[19]). India continued to expand the number of beneficiaries of its means-tested Pradhan Mantri Ujjwala Yojana liquefied petroleum gas (LPG) scheme, which was introduced in 2016 to support clean cooking facilities for families living below the poverty line. An additional 80 million households were added to the scheme (Pandey, 2019[20]). This jump made a major contribution to the record increase in India's LPG demand in 2019. Indonesia halted progress on the major fuel pricing reforms that have been implemented since 2015, freezing domestic fuel and electricity prices in 2018 to protect purchasing power from international oil price increases and a weak rupiah. The government increased its expenditure to compensate state-owned petroleum and electricity companies accordingly (OECD, 2019[21]).

The tendency for progress in deregulating fossil-fuel prices and rationalising subsidies to fluctuate in concert with global oil prices (Figure 1.3) underscores the need for governments to identify and pursue ways to effect truly durable reform, so that progress made in periods of low fuel prices endures when market, social or political parameters shift (see Chapter 2).

Figure 1.3. OECD-IEA combined estimates show a 19% decline in overall support from 2018 levels, driven by the impact of plunging oil prices on end-user subsidies

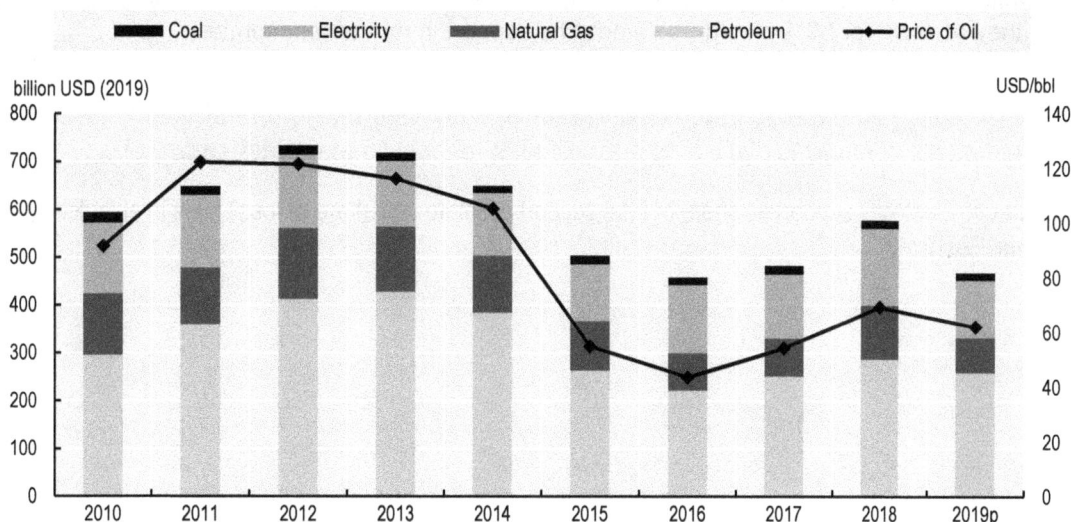

Source: OECD Inventory (2020), IEA Energy Subsidy data (2020).

End-use electricity support is substantial and rising

The Inventory documents substantial end-use electricity support – the fossil-fuel component of support enabling electricity companies to sell domestically generated electricity below market prices – in both the OECD and partner economies covered. Such support rose to USD 14 billion in 2019 up 7% from 2017.[11] Data on output-based support to the electricity sector have been included since the 2019 edition of the Inventory. The data complement information in previous editions on support for input fuels used in power generation, which continues to be counted under the relevant input fuel.[12] The data show that, unsurprisingly, support to end-use electricity is tied to a country's electricity generation mix (Figure 1.4).

Output-based support to the electricity sector in OECD member countries decreased by 13% from 2017 to 2019, mirroring the shift away from power generation fired by fossil fuels, particularly by coal, most notably in Europe (Section 1.1.1). OECD member countries' support for end-use electricity represents the least significant level of support across the four energy products covered in the Inventory. At USD 7 billion, it accounted for 7% of total support, compared with USD 72 billion for crude oil and refined petroleum products, USD 17 billion for natural gas and USD 9 billion for coal.

Nevertheless, several OECD member countries continue to provide support for fossil-fuel sourced electricity (Figure 1.4). Mexico, for example, has an electricity subsidisation programme that provides lower electricity prices for residential consumers, with direct budgetary transfers to its national electricity operator, the *Comisión Federal de Electricidad* (CFE). These transfers rose 21% between 2017 and 2019. Preliminary data for January-May 2020 indicate that this figure is likely to increase by around 60% in 2020 because COVID-19 mobility restrictions increased residential electricity consumption (Cantillo, 2020[22]). Mexico's direct subsidisation programme for electricity represented 27% of OECD member country end-use electricity support in 2019.

Italy and the United States (at state level) grant preferential value-added tax or sales tax rates for residential electricity consumption. The Netherlands provides end-use electricity support through direct budgetary transfers for its steel, aluminium, fertiliser and paper sectors, as indirect compensation under the European Union Emissions Trading System. Austria and Finland provide tax refunds for consumption by energy-intensive industry. Australia and Canada provide means-tested support for low-income residential consumers in sub-national jurisdictions, while measures in Greece target the Public Power Corporation's pensioners.

In contrast with the trend in OECD member countries, output-based support to the electricity sector in partner economies rose 47% between 2017 and 2019. This increase consisted mainly of direct budgetary outlays to compensate electricity operators for keeping electricity prices artificially low for end consumers. Indonesia and South Africa, in particular, have major electricity subsidisation programmes for predominantly coal-fired power generation (at least 75% of the national electricity generation mix). Together, they account for 80% of end-use electricity support in partner economies.

Figure 1.4. Countries with a high share of fossil fuels in the electricity generation mix tend to see an increased share of end-use electricity support with respect to their total support

Share of end-use electricity support as share of total support estimate and share of fossil fuels in electricity generation mix, 2019

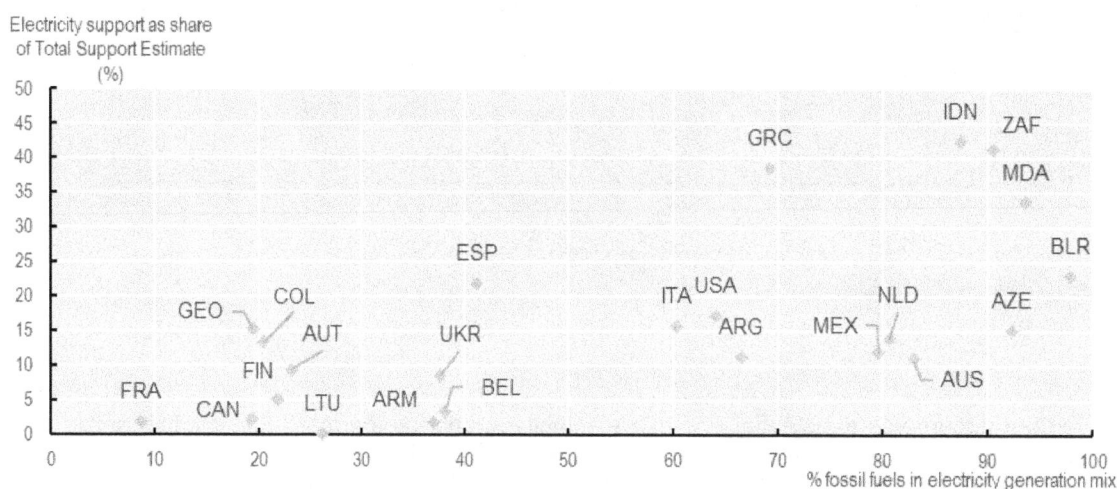

Note: ARG: Argentina, ARM: Armenia, AUS: Australia, AUT: Austria, AZE: Azerbaijan, BEL: Belgium, BLR: Belarus, CAN: Canada, COL: Colombia, ESP: Spain, FIN: Finland, FRA: France, GEO: Georgia, GRC: Greece, IDN   : Indonesia, ITA: Italy, LTU: Lithuania, MDA: Moldova, MEX: Mexico, NLD: Netherlands, UKR: Ukraine, USA: United States, ZAF: South Africa. No end-use electricity support for fossil fuels was recorded for the other 27 economies covered in the Inventory.
Sources: (OECD, 2020[1]), (IEA, 2020[10]).

1.1.3. The COVID-19 crisis and resulting oil price crash represent both a threat and an opportunity for reform

The COVID-19 crisis has led to a massive upheaval in the global energy system, both in terms of fuel prices and consumption. This upheaval is jeopardising reform of support for fossil fuels in some countries and strengthening reform in others.

The historic plunge in fossil-fuel prices will deepen the consumer support reductions of 2019 in countries that intervene to keep end-user prices artificially low, as the gap with market-based prices shrinks. Consumption subsidies are expected to fall to USD 181.9 billion in 2020 across the 42 economies covered by IEA price gap data (IEA, 2020[23]). This is down 43% from 2019 estimates and more than USD 100 billion from the previous low in 2016 (USD 287.2 billion).

Lower consumption also plays a role in reducing the estimate. Mobility restrictions introduced in response to COVID-19 significantly reduced transport activity and hence fuel consumption. Global energy demand is expected to fall by 5% in 2020, with oil consumption anticipated to decline by 8% and coal by 7% (IEA, 2020[24]). Lower fuel use will reduce in turn the consumption support reflected in the OECD Inventory, given that this support predominantly takes the form of preferential tax expenditures calculated per volumetric unit of fuel consumed; the lower the consumption, the less revenue forgone.

Low fuel prices also provide favourable socio-political conditions to pursue pricing reform – and therefore in theory more lasting reductions in support for fossil-fuel consumption than those resulting from international oil price reductions. Low prices minimise the impact of reform on consumers in net importing countries. In producer economies, declining government revenues can add impetus to reform, as pressure on public finances mounts. Yet governments' focus on providing immediate support to economies, firms and households affected by the COVID-19 response does not appear to have translated into widespread, additional momentum to use the opportunity that low fuel prices offer to advance pricing reform. Countries have taken diverging paths.

Nigeria, Africa's biggest producer of crude oil, announced in June that it would phase out petrol subsidies, saving USD 2 billion annually – a welcome boost as government coffers dwindle from the oil price crash and the country struggles to combat COVID-19 (Bala-Gbogbo, 2020[25]). Costa Rica and India have increased taxes on transport fuels, earmarking the increased revenue for measures to respond to COVID-19 (Wooders and Moerenhout, 2020[26]). Tunisia introduced a monthly price adjustment mechanism for gasoline and diesel in April 2020, to align pump prices with international fuel prices (Al Arabiya, 2020[27]).

However, other countries are enhancing price support, in particular for electricity consumers, including Armenia, Indonesia, Kazakhstan, Thailand and several African countries (IEA, 2020[23]). In response to the crisis, Indonesia committed IDR 15.4 trillion (Indonesian rupiahs) (USD 1.07 billion) from July through December 2020 to subsidise electricity use by lower-income households, small and medium-sized enterprises (SMEs) and certain industry categories (Suharsono and Lontoh, 2020[28]).

In addition, revenue decline from record low fuel prices can increase pressure on governments to intervene to bolster ailing industries, and in particular the fossil-fuel production sector, serving as a competing pull to reform efforts. The 2019 rise in support for fossil-fuel production is set to continue in 2020. Many countries are using stimulus measures for economies battered by the COVID-19 crisis to shore up fossil-fuel and related industries rather than prioritise sustainable investments and broader well-being objectives (OECD, 2020[29]) (Table 1.1). In doing so they are turning down major opportunities to align themselves with long-term emissions reduction goals (including those outlined in their own Nationally Determined Contributions to the Paris Agreement on climate change); to build resilience to climate change impacts; and to reduce the rate of biodiversity loss (OECD, 2020[30]).[13]

Table 1.1. Selected support measures for fossil-fuel producers announced or implemented as part of COVID-19 recovery packages

Country	Measure (date announced)	Total amount (USD)
Argentina	Introduction of oil price floor (USD 45/barrel) to prop up production and investment in Vaca Muerta shale field in northern Patagonia (May 2020)	N/a
	Four-year price subsidy programme for gas producers to revive Vaca Muerta and avoid jump in imports; companies to receive maximum of USD 3.70 per million British thermal units, with the government to cover the gap with current consumer prices (USD 2.30) (October 2020)	5.1 billion
Brazil	Reduction of royalties (up to 5%) for fields granted to small or medium-sized companies engaged in the exploration, development and production of oil and natural gas (July 2020)	N/a
Canada	Federal government budgetary transfer to the governments of Alberta, Saskatchewan and British Columbia, and to the Orphan Well Association, to clean up orphan and inactive oil and gas wells (April 2020)	1.3 billion
Indonesia	Cash compensation bailout for PT Pertamina (Persero) (oil and gas state-owned enterprise [SOE]) with support instalments through 2022 (May 2020)	3.12 billion
	Cash compensation and state capital injection for Perusahaan Listrik Negara (power utility SOE) for 2020 (May 2020)	2.51 billion
Mexico	Tax cut to state-controlled Pemex, decreasing Pemex's tax burden from 58% to 54% of profits (April 2020)	2.6 billion
Norway	Temporary oil and gas industry tax relief increasing deductions for new investments, to lower break-even prices for future exploration projects and fast-track new projects on the Norwegian continental shelf over the next two years (June 2020)	10.8 billion
United States	Royalty rate reductions for oil and gas operators with some states applying rates as low as 2.5% in lieu of the standard 12.5% royalty rate (April 2020)	N/a
	Competition for bids to establish coal product innovation centres, for manufacturing "value-added, carbon-based products from coal" and developing new methods for extraction and processing of "rare earth elements and critical minerals from coal" (July 2020)	122 million

Sources: (Mander, 2020[31]), (Wood Mackenzie, 2020[32]), (Gilbert, 2020[33]), (Belchior, Duarte and Leite, 2020[34]), (Presidência da República, 2020[35]), (Government of Canada, 2020[36]), (Government of Canada, 2021[37]), (IDN Financials, 2020[38]), (Webber, 2020[39]), (S&P Global Platts, 2020[40]), (Rystad Energy, 2020[41]), (Adomaitis and Solsvik, 2020[42]), (Brown, 2020[43]), (Meyer, 2020[44]), (Lefebvre, 2020[45]), (U.S. DOE, 2020[46]), (Matheson, 2020[47]), (Dlouhy, 2020[48]).

According to the Energy Policy Tracker initiative, a consortium of think tanks and universities, G20 governments have committed USD 428 billion[14] in energy support via new policies or policy amendments since the onset of the COVID-19 pandemic, with at least USD 235 billion going to fossil-fuel industries. Of that amount, USD 199 billion is characterised as "fossil unconditional" support, meaning that no climate change or pollution reduction requirements accompany policy measures. The Energy Policy Tracker consortium cautions that its estimates of support are necessarily only partial, extracted from only 3-5% of total government response commitments – those set out in official government sources (Energy Policy Tracker, 2020[49]). Incomplete government reporting represents a major obstacle to estimating support. Estimates are notably unable to routinely isolate and capture support to fossil-fuel industries delivered through "industry-neutral", cross-sector measures.[15] A more complete view of support is also hindered by difficulties in accessing quantitative estimates of tax expenditure measures and in putting a monetary figure on benefits conferred by regulatory roll-backs.

Broader studies confirm that recovery programmes or strategies have so far been weighted in favour of measures with a likely negative impact on the environment, rather than those promoting positive environmental outcomes (OECD, 2020[29]). For example, the Greenness of Stimulus Index compiled by the consultancy Vivid Economics identifies USD 3.7 trillion in G20 country stimulus support (of a total of USD 12 trillion) in favour of sectors with a significant and ongoing impact on nature as of October 2020, including the energy, transport and industry sectors. It finds that announced measures will have a "net negative" impact on the environment in 16 G20 economies.

The OECD supports and tracks COVID-19 recovery measures related to the environment

The OECD is helping governments to recover from the COVID-19 pandemic in ways that protect the environment and benefit everyone. This includes building resilience to future economic shocks and to accelerating environmental challenges (OECD, 2020[50]), and ensuring coherence between recovery measures and a broader set of economic, social and environmental goals (OECD, 2020[30]), (OECD, 2021[51]). The OECD has proposed 13 indicators to help governments measure the environmental impact of recovery measures and ensure recoveries are sustainable, including an indicator on reform of support for fossil fuels based on Inventory data (OECD, 2021[52]). The intention is to ensure recovery measures avoid entrenching market distortions that promote inefficiencies in energy production and use – along with polluting technologies – and that increase fossil fuel-intensive infrastructure and electricity (OECD, 2020[53]), (OECD, 2020[54]).

The OECD Inventory relies on official government documentation, like the Energy Policy Tracker, and is likely to face similar challenges in documenting support for fossil fuels channelled through economic recovery and stimulus packages. A majority of OECD country budgetary publications on revenue and expenditure are already published with a significant time lag, of two years or more. Mobility and work disruptions caused by the pandemic risk further increasing this delay, disrupting the operation of global statistical and data systems. The UN *Sustainable Development Goals Report* notes that out of 122 countries surveyed, 65% of national statistical offices are partially or fully closed, and 96% have partially or fully halted data collection (UN, 2020[55]). Furthermore, several COVID-19-related disbursements are of a limited, one-time nature, so there is a risk that they will not be recorded in official budgetary documents. The OECD is considering how best to address these risks, to ensure that future editions of the Inventory capture government support for fossil fuels as part of COVID-19 recovery and stimulus packages as comprehensively as possible.

1.1.4. Production and transport sectors dominate support measures

The transport and fossil-fuel production sectors received the largest shares of fossil-fuel support in OECD and partner economies taken as a whole in 2019, at around 30% of total support each (Figure 1.5). The 2020 Inventory includes sectoral breakdown of fossil-fuel support measures for the first time, across production and supply, energy transformation, and final consumption in transport, residential, and industry end-use sectors.[16] The intention is to provide an additional lens through which to assess government policies and budgets that include support for production and use of fossil fuels, consistent with the Inventory's objective to enhance transparency of the magnitude and nature of support policies (OECD, 2015[3]).

In OECD member countries, support for the fossil-fuel production sector represented 28% of total support. This large share reflects the considerable increase in support to fossil-fuel producers in 2018-19 (Section 1.1.1). Support to the production sector was also significant in partner economies (31%, compared with 32% for transport), reflecting the fact that fossil-fuel production forms a significant part of many of their economies. Azerbaijan, Brazil, Indonesia, the Russian Federation and South Africa are all net exporters of fossil fuels; Brazil, China and the Russian Federation fall among the top ten global oil producers and accounted for 20% of global production in 2019 (IEA, 2020[56]). Production sector support in partner economies mainly benefited petroleum (82%). Major contributing measures included:

- in Brazil, preferential tax treatment for fossil-fuel exploration and extraction;
- in India, customs duty exemptions on petroleum products sold at preferential domestic rates;
- in Indonesia, support to compensate SOEs for artificially low domestic prices;
- in the Russian Federation, a lower coefficient applied on the taxation of extracted crude oil.

China, India, Indonesia, the Russian Federation and South Africa are also prominent coal-producing countries, accounting for 72% of world coal production in 2019. Of partner economy producer support, 4% went to coal in 2019.

Figure 1.5. Transport and fossil-fuel production sectors dominate support measures

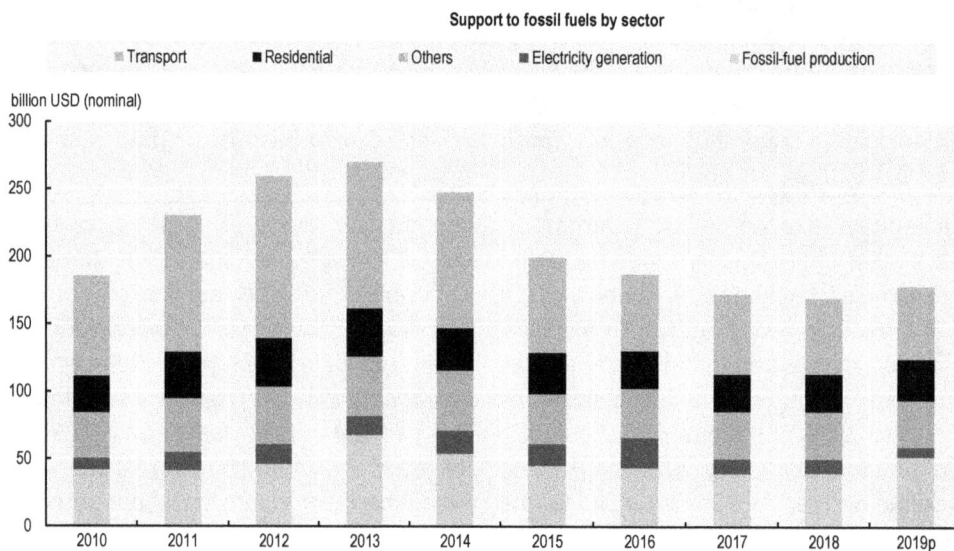

Support to fossil fuels by sector

Transport Residential Others Electricity generation Fossil-fuel production

Note: (i) USD in nominal value. (ii) Other sectors includes measures that support the use of fossil fuels in energy transformation other than electricity and heat generation: industrial and manufacturing; commercial and public services; agriculture, forestry and fisheries; and non-energy use.
Source: (OECD, 2020[1])

In OECD member countries, the high level of support for the transport sector might be expected, given that fuels used in road transport tend to be taxed at significantly higher rates than energy used in other sectors (OECD, 2019[57]) and that OECD member countries deliver 98% of their support in the sector through tax expenditures (Figure 1.6).[17] High nominal fuel excise taxes can translate into larger tax expenditures if tax concessions are in place, because preferential rates may then be well below benchmark rates (thus resulting in significant revenue forgone per measure). The OECD publication *Taxing Energy Use 2019*, which tracks progress in using energy and carbon taxes to encourage clean rather than polluting energy sources, finds that fuel excise taxes in the road sector drive effective carbon rates – that is, the sum of specific taxes on fossil fuels, carbon taxes and prices of tradable emission permits – in all 44 OECD and partner countries assessed (OECD, 2019[57]).

Across OECD member countries, however, the impact of nominal fuel excise taxes as a price signal is weakened by significant government support for the transport sector (29% of total government support). This suggests that it could be beneficial to undertake systematic, parallel analysis of nominal energy and carbon rates, and of country support for different users and fuels (including as documented in the Inventory), to integrate pricing and support measures. This would help to reveal the extent to which pricing signals represent a genuine boost to low-carbon incentives, as well as the coherence of government policy on meeting environmental goals (see Section 1.2.3). For the countries covered, *Taxing Energy Use 2019* undertakes much of this exercise, as it calculates energy tax rates net of tax expenditures and exemptions related to energy and carbon taxes. Future research would benefit from integrating relevant exemptions to broadly applicable taxes such as VAT or sales taxes, i.e. where they affect the difference in prices between energy sources.[18]

Non-OECD countries, for their part, support the transport sector more through direct budgetary outlays (57% in 2019) than through tax expenditures (43%) (Figure 1.6). The considerable fluctuations in partner economy support for the sector reflect in large part variations in transport fuel prices over time. Brazil, China and Indonesia made significant direct transfers to the road transport sector in 2018-19. Some of this was targeted support, such as preferential petroleum pricing in China for urban and rural passenger transport, or an emergency measure in Brazil in favour of the trucking sector. Indonesia, by contrast, directly subsidised diesel and petroleum to maintain artificially lower prices for general public consumption. Future research could usefully decompose price gap estimates to identify which shifts are due to genuine policy reform and which to price movements.

Figure 1.6. OECD member countries support fuels in the transport sector predominantly through tax expenditures, while partner economies favour direct budgetary transfers

Total support estimate benefiting transport sector, by support mechanism

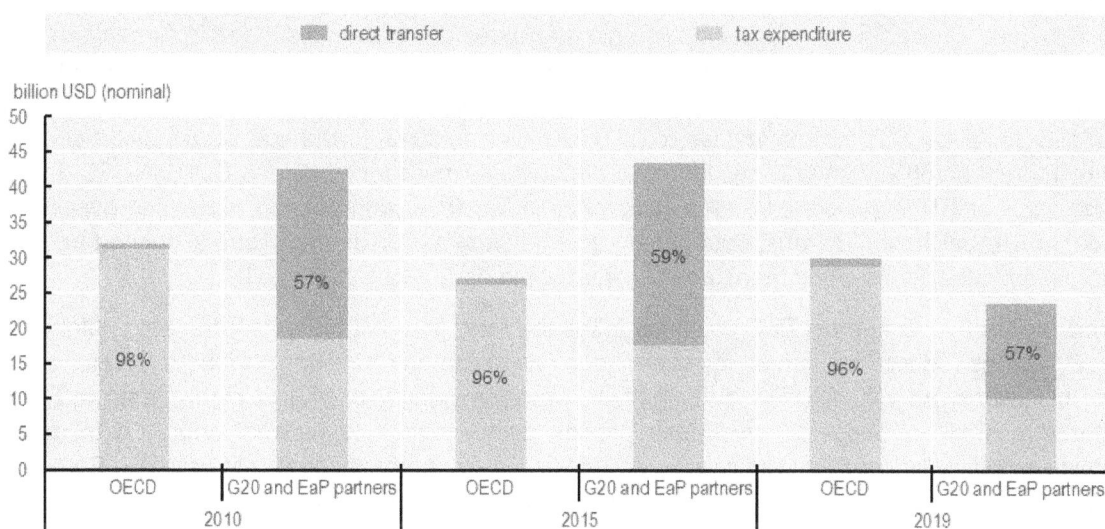

Source: (OECD, 2020[1])

The "other" sectors category, comprising industry and manufacturing, commercial and public services and energy transformation other than electricity and heat generation, also represents a large share (26%) of overall fossil-fuel support in OECD member countries. For EU member states, this reflects the fact that the EU Energy Taxation Directive enables imposition of preferential tax exemptions on the industrial, manufacturing and commercial sectors (European Commission, 2019[58]). With the notable exception of China, partner economies have smaller manufacturing and heavy industry sectors, so these sectors receive a smaller share of support. In addition, these countries tend to cross-subsidise household energy-use, with industry paying higher rates for energy than households.

The share of support for the residential sector has remained stable over the past decade, at 14%. In OECD member countries, the most significant measures are preferential fuel, sales or value-added taxes levied on residential heating fuels (e.g., natural gas, fuel oil, LPG), or on residential electricity end-use. Partner-economy support tends to take the form of direct budgetary outlays to compensate state-owned energy companies for losses resulting from artificially low energy prices, or for specific fuels destined for household use.

1.1.5. Support is declining in a majority of EU Eastern Partnership countries, but remains high relative to GDP

The inclusion of EU EaP countries as part of ongoing efforts to enhance the coverage of the Inventory enables assessment in the Companion for the first time of support in Armenia, Azerbaijan, Belarus, Georgia, Republic of Moldova and Ukraine.[19] Sixty-five direct budgetary transfers and tax expenditures were identified across the six countries, enhancing transparency on support for fossil fuels in a region where data availability on this issue has been limited.[20] The largest number of measures were identified in Ukraine (26), the fewest in Armenia (6).

The data reveal significant fluctuations in support levels across EaP countries in the past decade, as a considerable number of measures were eliminated and new ones introduced. Belarus terminated its VAT exemptions for natural gas, electricity and heat for residential consumers in early 2016, a measure with an annual worth of USD 200 million. Georgia introduced budgetary transfers to support natural gas for residential consumers in selected border regions, as well as an electricity subsidy programme for targeted residential groups (e.g. families with four or more children and other socially vulnerable groups). Ukraine recently eliminated several budgetary transfers, which will be replaced by measures to deal with emergencies and arrears in the energy sector.

Support is generally declining in Armenia, Georgia and Ukraine. Fossil-fuel support in Armenia peaked in 2013 and 2014 at USD 42 million and fell to USD 5 million in 2019 as a substantial number of support measures were removed. In Georgia, despite the implementation of new measures, support for fossil fuels fell to USD 15 million in 2019 from a peak of USD 33 million in 2013. In Ukraine, total support declined in 2019 by more than 50% from previous highs, but remained significant relative to GDP, at USD 2.2 billion (around 1.2% of GDP). No clear trend is discernible in Moldova, with support fluctuating over the past decade. In Azerbaijan and Belarus, data gaps prevent a clear assessment of general support trends, but in Azerbaijan, quantified support measures constituted almost 2% of GDP in 2018.

Support for fossil fuels in most EaP countries takes the form of direct budgetary transfers. Moldova, by contrast, applies reduced VAT rates for natural gas, electricity and heating provided to households and public institutions, as well as LPG consumption. Because energy pricing is highly regulated in EaP countries, most direct budgetary measures provide compensation to national energy companies for maintaining artificially low domestic energy prices, or aid in corporate debt restructuring. Some major measures target the end-use electricity sector, providing lower consumer electricity pricing on a means-tested basis or in selected geographic areas. The dominance of support for the residential sector implies that further analysis of support provided through below-market tariffs (i.e. induced transfers) is merited.[21]

Figure 1.7. Total support in EU Eastern Partnership countries fluctuated in the 2010s as some measures were eliminated and new measures introduced

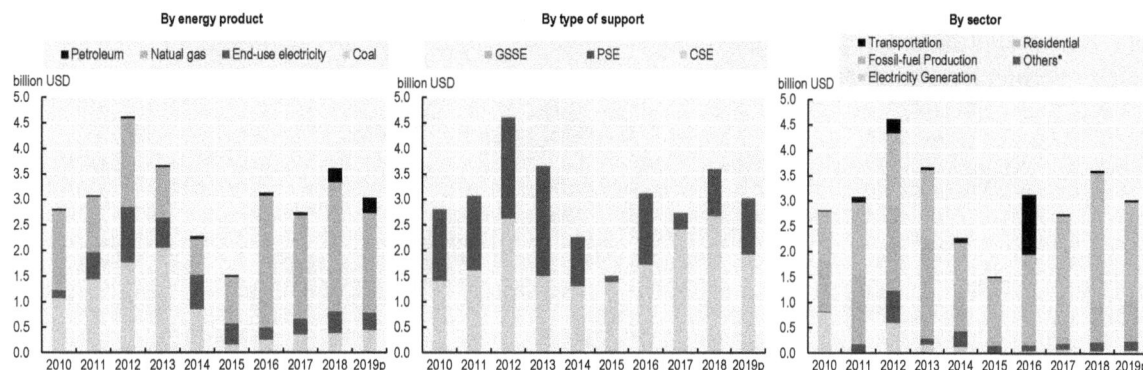

Note: USD in nominal value. (i) Support for electricity consumption refers to support for fossil-fuel powered electricity end-use (i.e. support for renewables and trade excepted). It excludes support to input fuels for electricity generation. (ii) PSE = production support estimate; CSE = consumer support estimate; GSSE = general services support estimate. (iii) Other sectors include measures that support the use of fossil fuels in energy transformation other than electricity and heat generation; industrial and manufacturing; commercial and public services; agriculture, forestry and fisheries; and non-energy use.
Source: (OECD, 2020[1])

1.1.6. A majority of countries provide ocean-related fossil-fuel support

Ocean-related fossil-fuel support measures have been put in place by at least 30 countries covered by the Inventory through 119 specific measures,[22] identified through a combination of automated and manual keyword searches on programme name, description and sector.[23] The 2020 Inventory identifies and tags support measures directly related to ocean sustainability as part of OECD efforts to mobilise expertise across policy fronts to support the transition to a more sustainable ocean economy. This new, OECD-wide initiative aims to meet the demands of the international community for a better evidence base to support decision making related to the sustainability of the ocean economy, the well-being and resilience of coastal communities, and the health of marine ecosystems. These measures are also reflected in the OECD's new Sustainable Ocean Economy database (OECD, 2020[59]), which brings together the OECD's ocean-related datasets and indicators, including through adaptations to existing datasets (such as the Inventory). Identifying ocean-related fossil-fuel support can help governments seeking to prioritise reform that promotes ocean sustainability.

Unsurprisingly, countries with extensive coastlines and maritime economic activities tend to have more ocean-related measures (Figure 1.8). Offshore oil and gas extraction are the main beneficiaries of ocean-related support in countries with significant fossil-fuel production, such as Australia, Brazil, the Russian Federation, the United Kingdom and the United States. Most of this is producer support (e.g. preferential tax treatment for offshore oil and gas extraction) and general services support (e.g. support for offshore research and exploration, or port infrastructure upgrades to increase trade capacity, Figure 1.9). The laying of pipelines, installation of offshore drilling rigs and discharge of contaminated water during the petroleum extraction process are all detrimental to marine ecosystems, as are potential oil spills and noise generated by drilling stations.

Norway stands as an exception among producer economies: despite being a major offshore oil and gas producer, most of its ocean-related support measures are targeted at the transport sector and the fisheries and aquaculture sector. Countries with little or no domestic fossil-fuel production tend to follow a similar pattern to Norway, providing support via preferential tax rates on fuels used in fisheries and aquaculture, or support for fossil-fuel consumption in maritime transport (Figure 1.8). Such measures potentially exacerbate overfishing and encourage excessive marine fleet traffic, and increase the risk of coral reef destruction by ship anchors and stranded ships.

Figure 1.8. Ocean-related support measures benefit both production and consumption, led by countries with extensive coastlines and marine economic activities

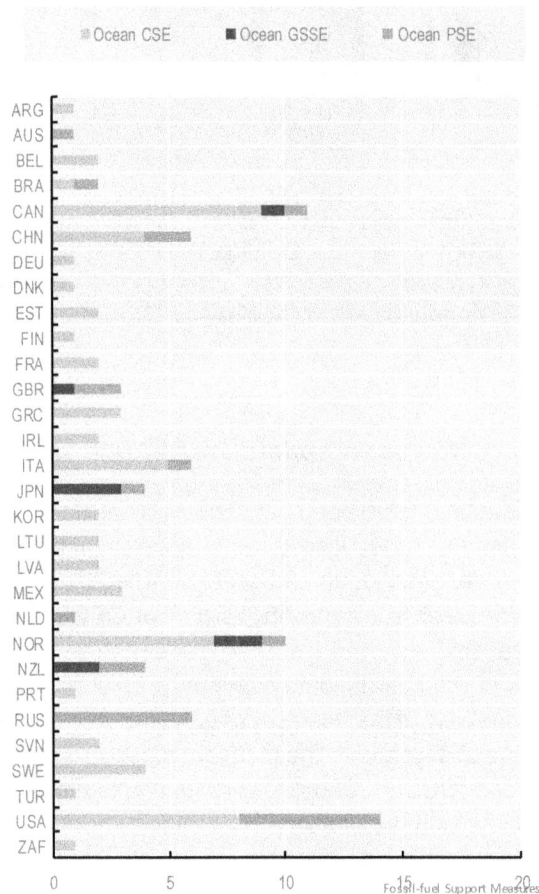

Note: Includes measures for which disbursement of funds were observed at least once between 2015 and 2017 as well as ongoing fossil-fuel support measures for which no data were available. Only active measures are included, with measures terminated by 2017 excluded. For federated countries, most of the identified ocean-related support measures are sub-national and applicable only in certain coastal regions of a country (e.g., Alaska, California, Louisiana and Texas in the United States; British Columbia, Labrador, New Brunswick and Newfoundland in Canada). Figures for Canada, China and the United States include both federal (central government) and sub-national measures.
Source: (OECD, 2020[1]).

Figure 1.9. Offshore oil and gas is the main beneficiary of ocean--related fossil-fuel support in most producer countries; transport, fishing, and aquaculture end users benefit most elsewhere

Sectoral percentages of ocean-related fossil-fuel support

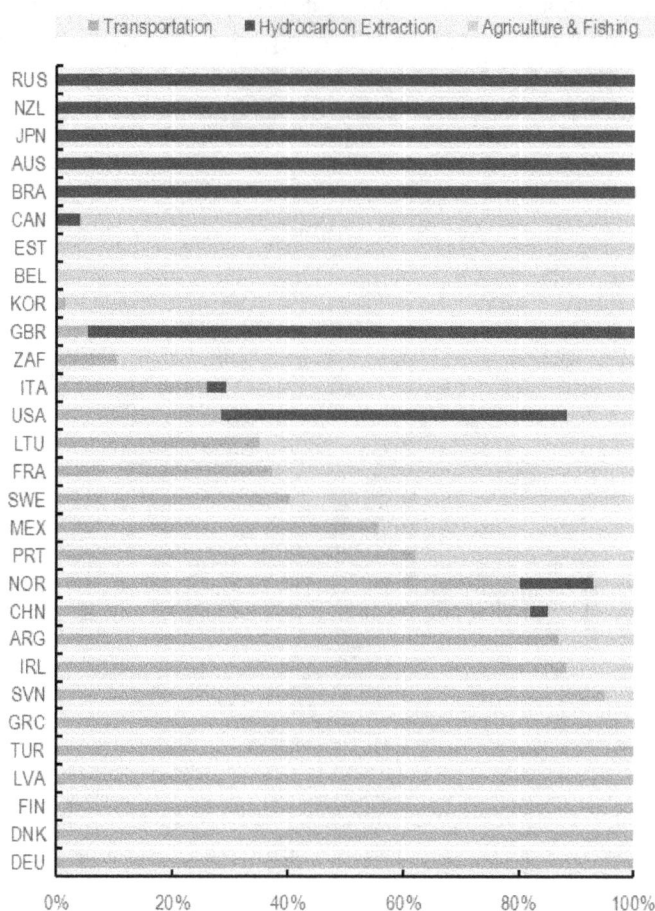

Note: The proportion of support benefiting end-user sectors is calculated using the median of ocean-related fossil-fuel support measures with active fund disbursements in 2015-2017. These disbursements (targeting specific known fuels) are allocated to sectors using country-level sectoral energy consumption data from the IEA World Energy Balances. See Annex A.
Source: (OECD, 2020[1]).

1.2. Developments in tracking and monitoring fossil-fuel support

1.2.1. G20 peer reviews are generating lessons about good practice in reform of fossil-fuel subsidies

G20 leaders reaffirmed their joint commitment to rationalise and phase out "inefficient fossil-fuel subsidies that encourage wasteful consumption" over the medium term, while ensuring targeted support for the poorest, in the Riyadh Leaders' Declaration of 22 November 2020 (G20, 2020[60]). First made at the Pittsburgh G20 summit in 2009, this commitment has been reiterated at subsequent summits.[24] Nevertheless, support levels remain similar to 2010 levels, having increased substantially to 2013 then receded in the interim (Figure 1.10). Since 2013, G20 countries have developed and implemented a framework for voluntary, reciprocal peer reviews of inefficient fossil-fuel support "as a valuable means of enhanced transparency and accountability" (G20, 2013[61]).

Three sets of paired peer reviews have been conducted so far: China and the United States (completed 2016), Germany and Mexico (completed 2017), and Indonesia and Italy (completed 2019). Argentina and Canada announced their intention to undertake a reciprocal peer review in conjunction with the G20 Energy Transitions Ministerial Meeting in June 2018 in Bariloche, Argentina; this process is still under way. France and India signalled their intent to follow suit as the next peer review pair during an official visit to France by Prime Minister Narendra Modi in August 2019. G20 energy ministers have encouraged all G20 members yet to initiate a peer review process to do so as soon as feasible (G20, 2018[62]).[25] Several economies have undertaken similar peer reviews under the umbrella of the Asia-Pacific Economic Cooperation (APEC) forum.[26]

Figure 1.10. Measures benefiting petroleum, consumers and the transport sector remain the dominant form of support in G20 economies

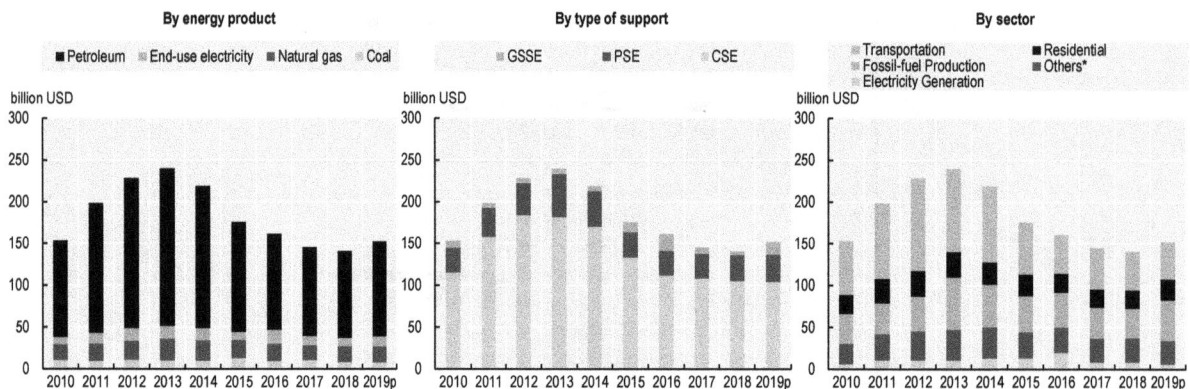

Note: USD in nominal value. (i) The graph above represents the arithmetic sum of the following partner G20 economies: Argentina, Australia, Brazil, Canada, China, France, Germany, India, Indonesia, Italy, Japan, Republic of Korea, Mexico, Russia, South Africa, Turkey, the United Kingdom and the United States. Saudi Arabia is omitted due to absence of data. (ii) Support for electricity consumption refers to support for fossil-fuel powered electricity end-use (i.e. support from renewables and trade excepted). It excludes support to input fuels for electricity generation. (iii) PSE = production support estimate; CSE = consumer support estimate; GSSE = general services support estimate. (iv) Other sectors include measures that support the use of fossil fuels in energy transformation other than electricity and heat generation; industrial and manufacturing; commercial and public services; agriculture, forestry and fisheries; and non-energy use.
Source: (OECD, 2020[1]).

The G20 peer reviews complement periodic self-reporting by G20 countries on fossil-fuel subsidies that they deem inefficient. Neither process has produced a common definition of the meaning of "inefficient fossil-fuel subsidies that encourage wasteful consumption", but a degree of precedent on the process for conducting the peer reviews has emerged from those reviews undertaken so far (OECD and IEA, 2019[63]) and (OECD, 2018[2]). Preliminary steps include agreeing to the terms of reference on the scope of measures to be reviewed and the review timeline, and selecting a review panel. Panels have traditionally been composed predominantly of G20 member economies, along with the OECD. In subsequent steps, the country under review produces an initial self-report to provide context on the implementation of the measures under review and potential avenues for reform or phase-out. Exchanges with the review team on the draft, by written comment and in-person meetings, are followed by development and agreement of a final report, which includes suggestions by the peer review panel.[27] The OECD Secretariat has chaired the review process and led drafting of the final report for all six completed peer reviews.

The terms of reference developed by peer review countries have explicitly flagged sharing lessons and experience of relevant reform as a main purpose of G20 peer reviews. The reviews shine a light on the economic and environmental motivations for reform of support for fossil fuels (OECD and IEA, 2019[63]) (OECD, 2018[2]). They provide examples of successful reform and of challenges associated with it, underscoring the importance of complementary social support policies to cushion any adverse impacts on vulnerable populations or on industry competitiveness. The process encourages countries under review to carefully dissect the rationale behind support policies and determine whether that rationale still holds, whether it could be met more effectively or efficiently by other means, and how support policies might be reformed or phased out. The peer review process tends to generate more information about country support policies than periodic self-reporting, encouraging countries to improve their ability to measure and track support policies, and signalling a commitment to transparency. It can also be a beneficial learning experience for the countries under review and for the peer reviewers, and represents an important vehicle for knowledge exchange. Finally, the peer reviews promote cross-ministerial co-ordination and reflection on policy coherence and complementarities.

Over 100 government policies have been evaluated across the peer reviews conducted to date, two-thirds of which benefit end users of fossil fuels. They comprise predominantly tax expenditures, but also direct budgetary measures and, in a couple of instances, risk transfer mechanisms (Table 1.2).

Table 1.2. Summary of G20 peer reviews

G20 Member State	Date of completion	Peer review panel	Number and self-declared value of measures reviewed (where quantified)	Transfer mechanisms	Beneficiaries	Main suggestions of the peer review panel
China	2016	Germany, Indonesia, United States, International Monetary Fund, OECD (chair)	9 measures, USD 15.5 billion (2016)	Direct budgetary transfers (1 set), tax expenditures (8)	Measures span the fossil-fuel supply chain, from upstream exploration and development of fossil-fuel resources to refining and their use in power and heat generation, transport, and the residential sector.	Reform fossil-fuel subsidies as a necessary step towards the goal of more market-based prices and taxes that better reflect environmental damage from economic activities, thereby contributing to pollution reduction while removing one major source of price distortions in the economy. Continue efforts to ensure that the most vulnerable segments of society are not adversely affected by reform. To enhance transparency of fossil-fuel subsidies: • Enhance information on fossil-fuel subsidies, their environmental effects, and their beneficiaries to facilitate identification of necessary reforms and more efficient policies. • Encourage provinces to provide information and data on support measures (at least to the same degree as that available for central government level). • Improve and provide information on taxes applicable to energy producers and consumers, and relevant tax revenues, to enhance understanding of potential fiscal gains from reform. • Provide more information on rules used to set energy prices, where still regulated. Ensure price reform goes beyond eliminating the identified fossil-fuel subsidies, to capture environmental consequences of production and consumption of fossil fuels through efficient pricing.
Germany	2017	China, Indonesia, Mexico, Italy, New Zealand, United States, OECD (chair)	22 measures, EUR 15 billion (USD 17.9 billion)	Direct budgetary transfers (2), tax expenditures (20)	Bulk of measures are energy and electricity tax preferences for agriculture, manufacturing and	Assess the sensitivity of industry competitiveness and carbon leakage to reform (quantify effects on volumes of production, trade and price, and

G20 Member State	Date of completion	Peer review panel	Number and self-declared value of measures reviewed (where quantified)	Transfer mechanisms	Beneficiaries	Main suggestions of the peer review panel
			(2016)		transport sectors; 2 measures favour upstream activities (extraction of coal).	therefore GDP, and associated environmental and social costs), to test the assertion that tax benefits granted to industrial and agriculture sectors ensure the competitiveness of German industry and prevent carbon leakage (and are therefore not "inefficient"): • Carry out periodic quantitative assessments of competitiveness and carbon leakage effects of energy-tax preferences, including state-of-the-art empirical evidence. • Improve data on sectoral distribution of beneficiaries of support measures. • Publish more detailed information on energy efficiency performance of industries and distribution of tax benefits corresponding to performance. • Review support measures to ascertain role in energy transition. Consider alternative, less distortive measures, to help maintain industry competitiveness and prevent emissions relocation, lighten environmental and social costs incurred, and help ensure economic and climate policy objectives are aligned.
Indonesia	2019	China, Germany, Italy, Mexico, New Zealand, German Corporation for International Co-operation (GIZ), IEA, International Institute for Sustainable Development (IISD), OECD (chair), World Bank	12 measures, USD 9 billion (2016)	Direct budgetary transfers (5); tax expenditures (7)	Two main categories of beneficiaries: end users of petroleum fuels and electricity, and oil and gas industry upstream and downstream segments (preferential tax treatment for exploration, development and extraction, and refining and processing).	Continue petroleum fuel and electricity pricing reform by harnessing socio-economic information in the unified poverty database (which gathers socioeconomic information on the poorest households), to provide targeted support to poor households and establish a fiscally sustainable energy access policy. Enhance data collection to better understand the behavioural impacts of pricing reforms on consumption, health, and congestion. In addition to focusing on reducing the number of beneficiaries of subsidised electricity and LPG cylinders, decouple social support from fossil-fuel consumption as a longer-term goal (e.g. through

G20 Member State	Date of completion	Peer review panel	Number and self-declared value of measures reviewed (where quantified)	Transfer mechanisms	Beneficiaries	Main suggestions of the peer review panel
						means-tested cash transfers). Avoid the erosion of reform by political intervention (e.g. government deviation from automatic adjustments in fuel prices, maintenance of fixed fuel and electricity prices to the end of 2019 to shield citizens from increasing international oil prices/weakening rupiah), which increases the likelihood of potential losses by state-owned fuel and electricity companies and fiscal pressure on government, and appears incoherent with overall energy and climate policy. Develop a comprehensive inventory of fossil-fuel support measures and associated costs to government, including direct transfers, preferential tax treatment and government credit assistance. Systematically measure tax incentives that encourage national production of crude oil, natural gas and refined petroleum products (for which no reform plans exist) and planned expansion of tax incentives to industrial users of fossil fuels (longer duration, increasing eligible sectors, simplified application procedures), to foster greater transparency and accountability, ensure measures achieve objectives in the most cost-effective way, and eventually facilitate reform. Assess how incentives to fossil-fuel producers might distort exploration, development and extraction decisions, and result in support for fossil fuels. Isolate data on transport and distribution costs for fuels by region to help indicate the extent of cross-subsidisation resulting from the "one price policy" harmonising energy prices across regions.
Italy	2019	Argentina, Canada, Chile, China, France, Germany, Indonesia, Netherlands, New Zealand, Bocconi	39 measures, EUR 13 billion (USD 15.5 billion)	Tax expenditures (35); Direct budgetary spending (4) (and 1 risk transfer mechanism,	Heterogeneous set of measures (e.g. targeting households, energy producers, public services), inventoried by main benefiting sector	Enhance the existing catalogue of environmentally harmful and environmentally friendly subsidies: • Indicate distributional impacts of inventoried

G20 Member State	Date of completion	Peer review panel	Number and self-declared value of measures reviewed (where quantified)	Transfer mechanisms	Beneficiaries	Main suggestions of the peer review panel
		University, IEA, IISD, European Energy Retailers, Green Budget Europe, OECD (chair), University of Pavia, UN Environment	(2016)	Export Credit Guarantees for coal, gas-fired and nuclear power plants in third countries, not quantified)	(energy, industry, transport, households and public services, and agriculture). Transport benefits from more than half of amounts estimated, and more than a quarter of measures (11).	measures. • Report available evidence on environmental and health impacts of fossil fuels and their relationship with subsidy levels, and potentially evaluate cost implications for the economy; add regional- and city-level surveys. • Analyse support mechanisms other than direct budgetary and tax expenditure measures. • Describe the initially intended objective of support measures, details on delivery mechanisms, assess quantitative value and whether objectives are met. Publish and disseminate widely the results of novel inclusion of macroeconomic assessment of fossil-fuel support phase-out (CGE modelling) in self-review report, to inform public debate. Prioritise measures for reform (e.g. measures whose intended policy objective is defunct, or that are not efficiently meeting their objectives): • Eliminate direct subsidies and tax expenditures allocated to fossil-fuel producers or distributers that are not fulfilling any desired policy objectives efficiently. • Phase out longstanding subsidies targeted at particular industries and not aligned with current social needs and policy objectives (e.g. subsidies to taxis, magnesium production from seawater, public services). • Consider reducing or eliminating differences in the rates of excise taxation on diesel and gasoline. • Develop detailed plans for phasing out major tax expenditures on road freight transport, maritime transport, aviation and agriculture that are inefficient. Assess potential equity, poverty and competitiveness impacts, and possible transition

G20 Member State	Date of completion	Peer review panel	Number and self-declared value of measures reviewed (where quantified)	Transfer mechanisms	Beneficiaries	Main suggestions of the peer review panel
						measures. Accompany reform with a well-designed communication strategy.
Mexico	2017	China, Germany, Indonesia, Italy, New Zealand, United States, OECD (chair)	10 measures, USD 26 billion (2016)	Direct budgetary transfers (for fossil fuels used in transport, agricultural and fishing activities); tax expenditures	Producer support (1 measure); downstream support for fossil fuels used in transport; and farmers, fishing vessels, or public transport.	To finalise energy-sector reforms, fully liberalise diesel and gasoline prices, and further stimulate competition in the energy sector, ensuring a high-level of transparency and regulatory certainty. Consider using additional revenues raised from reformed taxes for social compensation measures to address any distributional impacts of changes to taxes or subsidies. Address the problem of high levels of tax avoidance and evasion associated with informal coal operations. Consider increasing the recently introduced carbon tax to better reflect the social costs of carbon and the different fuels' respective carbon contents (in view of coal being taxed at much lower rates than other fuels, and natural gas being fully exempted from the carbon tax). Consider the impact of support for electricity consumption (currently considered a different, although linked issue from fossil-fuel subsidies) on the demand for natural gas, petroleum products and coal, as likely indirectly increasing final consumption of fossil fuels. Review fuel-tax concessions (reduced energy excise tax for fishers and farmers; carbon tax exemptions and reductions) – not currently considered subsidies by Mexico – recognising that they could be leading to more consumption and pollution than would have otherwise been the case, and perhaps causing other distortions. Look for alternative and less distortive ways of benefiting the targeted activities.
United States	2016	China, Germany, Mexico, OECD (chair)	17 measures, USD 8.2 billion (2016);	Direct budgetary transfer (1), tax expenditures (15),	Upstream activities (exploration, development and extraction),	Pursue reform of the 16 measures identified as "inefficient" in the US self-report on the grounds that

G20 Member State	Date of completion	Peer review panel	Number and self-declared value of measures reviewed (where quantified)	Transfer mechanisms	Beneficiaries	Main suggestions of the peer review panel
			value of liability cap on natural resource damage not quantified	risk transfer mechanism (1)	grouped in the peer review report according to the branch of government responsible for reform. Focus on federal subsidies to hydrocarbons and coal (i.e. not all possible forms of fossil-fuel subsidies). 1 measure supporting fossil-fuel use in the residential sector.	their original purpose was found to be outdated or inappropriate. Improve the existing reporting process, make necessary reforms easier to identify and engender more efficient policies by: • encouraging states to provide at least the same degree of transparency and information that applies to federal measures • undertaking research on the beneficiaries of subsidies, improving data and understanding of environmental impacts of subsidies • encouraging further research into possible support not identified in the course of the review (e.g. preferential loan-guarantees, investment incentives, regulations favouring fossil-fuel producers or fossil-fuel-based power generators). Dedicate additional effort to convincing citizens of the need for fossil-fuel subsidy reform, to contribute to pollution reduction while removing an important source of price distortion, and facilitate the passage of reform measures through Congress. Take price reform beyond eliminating subsidies, to move towards internalising the environmental damage that arises from the production and consumption of fossil fuels through efficient energy taxation. Reassess the financing structure of inland waterways, in particular the levels of user fees and fuel excise taxes: the costs of constructing, operating and maintaining inland waterways are largely borne by the taxpayer, and more than half of the volume of freight transported concerns fossil fuels, but no subsidy for bulk transportation of fossil fuels by rail and barges was identified in the peer review.

Notes: (1). Argentina and Canada announced their intention to undertake the peer review process in June 2018. After national elections in both countries in October 2019 and a change of administration in Argentina, the peer review process for this pair will likely conclude in 2021. (2). France and India announced that they would move forward with a peer review under the auspices of the G20 during an official visit to France by PM Modi in August 2019; the process remains in a preliminary phase. (3). The recommendations made by the peer review panel in the Italian peer review respond specifically to a request by the Italian authorities to offer suggestions for how to structure the country's fossil-fuel subsidy reform process.

Source: G20 peer reviews, available at **www.oecd.org/fossil-fuels/publication/**.

A common issue that emerges from the discussion in the peer reviews is the challenge of defining what constitutes an "inefficient fossil-fuel subsidy that encourages wasteful consumption" for the purposes of the overarching G20 commitment. The G20 has not adopted a formal definition of any of the three elements of the reform mandate – what constitutes a fossil-fuel subsidy, what kind of measures might be deemed inefficient or what can be considered wasteful consumption.[28] The peer-review process is country-led, which means that reviewed countries themselves identify which policies to subject to review and which support measures they propose to reform – and therefore which measures might be considered inefficient and encouraging wasteful consumption. Nevertheless, the process provides an important first step towards a possible future common definition by shedding light on differences in interpretation between reviewed countries on what should be considered an inefficient subsidy.

For example, Germany and Mexico adopted different definitions of subsidies for their peer review process. Germany's definition covered direct budgetary transfers and tax expenditures (Steenblik et al., 2017[64]), while Mexico's referred only to direct budgetary transfers – although its self-report nevertheless included discussion on tax expenditures (Steenblik et al., 2017[65]). China (Steenblik et al., 2016[66]), Germany and Italy (Steenblik et al., 2019[67]) included in fossil-fuel subsidies those providing support to fossil fuel-based electric power production and consumption; Mexico and the United States did not. Italy classed every subsidy to fossil-fuel production and consumption as inefficient, including 39 measures in its self-review. China and the United States signalled their intent to phase out specified measures benefiting fossil-fuel production, recognising that the reduction in prices resulting from these measures encouraged "wasteful consumption". Germany offered a similar motivation for reform of measures propping up domestic hard-coal production.

Peer review panels have also provided commentary on countries' definitions of the terms, interpreting their mandate as going beyond merely documenting those definitions. For example, the panel in the German review questioned Germany's assertion that industry support measures were efficient because they were aimed at maintaining the competitiveness of German industry and avoiding carbon leakage to countries with less-stringent environmental regulations. The panel noted to properly distinguish subsidies that might enhance the well-being of an economy from inefficient subsidies, it would be necessary to weigh their social costs and benefits, assessing not only the design of relevant fuel-tax exemptions and reductions compared with alternatives, but also whether they were periodically adjusted to reflect changing priorities and circumstances. The panel recommended that Germany assess the sensitivity of industry competitiveness and carbon leakage to fossil-fuel subsidy reform and possible (potentially less distortive) alternatives, to test the assertion of the "efficiency" of these measures, and set out a number of potential steps to this end. The panel highlighted a lack of consensus in international literature on the impact of environmental regulation on firm and industry performance.

The panel for the Mexican review noted that Mexico did not consider any of its tax exemptions and reductions in support of consumption as inefficient (and therefore in need of reform), because they did not decrease prices below marginal costs. The panel pointed to the fact that the term "inefficient" as used by many G20 members covers such measures. China and the United States, for example, reported "mainly features of their tax codes that favoured fossil-fuel producers" as inefficient measures for reform. The panel noted that by taking into account solely the burden on welfare of taxing energy products, Mexico failed to take into account the welfare impact of environmental consequences of fossil-fuel consumption, or the impact of the reductions or exemptions in question on the overall efficiency of the tax system. Panel members urged Mexico to review fuel-tax concessions to see whether they were increasing consumption and pollution levels, and leading to other distortions. They also encouraged Mexico to include support for the use of fossil fuels for electricity generation when assessing electricity subsidy reform priorities. The overarching conclusion of peer review panels has been that further dialogue on definitions could help G20 member states reach agreement on what should be considered an inefficient subsidy for the purposes of the G20 reform commitment.

Analysis in the peer reviews also provides insight into how countries might go about the reform process. The peer review on Italy, for example, provided several suggestions for the structuring and sequencing of reform, and possible reform measures, after the Italian government requested help in identifying priorities for phasing out subsidies. The review team canvassed literature on international experience with reform and noted that identifying subsidy measures, their intended objective and whether this is being met, and how measures are delivered (e.g. direct transfers, tax incentives, transfer of risk to government, induced transfers), are first steps to formulating a comprehensive and coherent reform effort. Determining the quantitative value of support measures is also essential, ideally through a complete cost-benefit analysis or, if that is not feasible, through estimates or qualitative discussion of budgetary cost, as well as impacts on households, firms, the environment and public health. The panel commended existing efforts by Italy to enhance transparency on environmentally related subsidies and their impact through a regularly updated Catalogue of Environmentally Harmful and Environmentally Friendly Subsidies, specifying budgetary cost and rationale for implementation of measures in most cases, as well as the inclusion in Italy's self-review of a model-based macroeconomic assessment of the impact of possible phase-out of support measures. The reviewers nevertheless made several suggestions to enhance the value of the catalogue. The panel proposed that the results of the macroeconomic assessment be widely publicised to support public debate on reform.

Once fossil-fuel support measures have been identified and quantified as much as possible, measures for reform need to be prioritised. Eliminating all measures in a single "big bang" reform could have major economic and social impacts, and be technically and politically difficult. The review panel suggested ways to set reform priorities. These ranged from removing measures that no longer serve a valid policy objective or efficiently meet their intended objective, to searching for more effective, alternative measures to reach intended policy aims, and assessing and addressing possible impacts of reform on equity or poverty. The review team then tailored these approaches to the Italian context, to make specific recommendations on possible measures for reform.

The Italian example is unusual. Reviewed countries generally propose reform options in their self-reports to frame review panel discussions. This approach reflects the recognition of reform as a sovereign issue tied to country-specific circumstances and priorities. However, other peer review reports also touch on ways reviewed countries might enhance and accelerate reform processes. For example, the China review team praised the notable transparency of the China self-review report as an "unprecedented, government-led look at policies supporting the production and consumption of fossil fuels in China". It nevertheless highlighted several ways China could build on that progress to further improve reporting on subsidies, their effects and their beneficiaries, and thereby make it easier to identify needed reforms and enhance policy efficiency. Similarly, the panel in the United States review (Steenblik et al., 2016[68]) made several suggestions about how the country might improve existing processes, including by seeking to enhance understanding of support measures not addressed in the peer review, and improving efforts to convince citizens of the need for reform as a means to help steer reform measures through Congress. Chapter 2 of this report builds in part on the advice in G20 peer reviews to set out in detail how governments might adopt a robust sequential approach to designing fossil-fuel subsidy reforms.

A further lesson arising from G20 peer reviews is that reform processes can be vulnerable to the prevailing political environment. The panel reviewing Indonesia, for example, commended the Indonesian government for 2014-17 reforms to fuel and electricity subsidies, noting that they brought the country's energy prices more into line with international oil price movements and generated significant savings for reallocation to other government priorities (e.g. social and infrastructure programmes) (OECD, 2019[21]). But the team also noted recent erosions to fuel pricing reform efforts, including a 2018 presidential order to hold prices stable despite rising international oil prices, to preserve purchasing power and sustain growth (Suzuki and Nakano, 2018[69]). The review panel said the pending presidential election was "not inconsequential" to the policy revisions, and cautioned against possible renewed fiscal pressure, reinforced energy price distortions and further encouragement for wasteful consumption, noting a jump in energy subsidies for kerosene, LPG and electricity of almost IDR 50 trillion (USD 3.5 billion) from 2016 to 2018 (IDR 106.8 trillion to IDR 153.5 trillion). The panel team observed that these developments underlined the political environment as a "major deciding factor for the resilience of reforms". The peer review report on China also flags the risk of subsidy reinstatement spurred by fuel-price increases (or conversely that of enhanced support for producers in times when crude-oil prices slump), noting the need for continued monitoring by the G20 and other organisations, and ongoing efforts to improve transparency of support.

Examples of good practice in reform: transitioning industry, "pro-poor" reform, fuel price liberalisation

In addition to setting out several "scalable" lessons emerging from country experience, the peer review reports highlight examples of good practice that could inform efforts to phase out fossil-fuel support in other countries. The team reviewing Germany, for example, identified the country's experience in phasing out subsidies to the hard-coal mining industry over several decades as a notable successful reform. The team pointed to several elements of the German process that could be of interest to other countries, including consolidation of industry under a single umbrella company to manage legacy debts and liabilities, and restoration efforts; a series of industry stakeholder meetings conducted over several years to plan the scale-back of industry; and successful workforce retraining and relocation. A strong emphasis on retraining younger workers for relocation meant that no lay-offs resulted from mine closures, which greatly assisted the social acceptability of reform.

The panel reviewing Indonesia highlighted efforts to better target electricity subsidies as a good example of "pro-poor" subsidy reform. The government had been subsidising electricity prices for a majority of consumers as a means to help alleviate poverty, address inequality and enhance energy access, with support reaching a high of USD 9 billion in 2013-14, as international oil prices spiked. The rising costs of the electricity subsidy scheme and an acknowledgement of poor targeting led the government to begin reform in 2013, to try to focus support on low-income households. As a first step, the government phased out support for 12 consumer classes across industry, business, government and residential groups between 2013 and 2016, focusing on consumers with the largest power connections. Then, the government sought to better target support for the two most vulnerable residential classes at the end of 2016, to isolate "poor" 450 volt-ampere (VA) and 900 VA households (the bottom 40% of households) from "non-poor", by using a new united poverty database of socioeconomic information on vulnerable households. The number of supported 900 VA consumers dropped dramatically, from 23 million to 4 million, yielding significant savings for government. The cost of electricity subsidies fell to USD 3.4 billion in 2017, from USD 8.6 billion in 2014.

The review team praised Indonesia's accomplishment in reducing electricity subsidy expenditure and developing the tools needed to better target subsidies, in the form of the united poverty database and a smart card system for both electricity and LPG subsidies. It nevertheless pointed out that Indonesia could further improve the targeting of support and remedy distributional problems raised by universal subsidies by decoupling subsidies from consumption, for example by favouring means-tested cash transfers .

The team reviewing Mexico, for its part, championed the country's achievement in fuel pricing and taxation reform as "remarkable" and holding "valuable lessons for other emerging economies wishing to carry out a broad-based reform of the energy sector" (Steenblik et al., 2017[65]). The review team noted the fundamental shift in fuel pricing policies starting in 2013, from heavy support for gasoline, diesel and LPG to net positive taxes through reform of the IEPS, a floating excise tax (Impuesto Especial sobre Producción y Servicios por Enajenación de Gasolina y Diesel). The market for LPG became fully liberalised at the beginning of 2017. The panel urged Mexico to build on this success by continuing on its path towards full liberalisation of diesel and gasoline prices.

Building on progress to date

To build on progress to date, G20 countries could track and share more systematically the lessons and experience of reform generated by the peer review process. A more structured platform could better disseminate outcomes and follow-up of review processes and a compendium of good practice arising from peer reviews could be developed. More systematic follow-up would support reform efforts not only within the G20 but also beyond.

The Netherlands is an example of a country that recently underwent a peer review of its efforts to phase out support for fossil fuels inspired by the G20 reviews, as an Invited Guest Country under G20 presidencies and having sat on the peer review panel for the Italian review (2019). The outcome of the process, which was facilitated by the OECD and the IEA, was presented to the Dutch Parliament on 14 September 2020 as an important resource to shed light on support for fossil fuels, enhance accountability on public expenditure and identify opportunities for reform (Elgouacem and Journeay-Kaler, 2020[70]). It was also used to expand the scope of fossil-fuel subsidies referenced in the final National Climate and Energy Plan of the Netherlands delivered to the European Commission at the end of 2019.[29] A more systematic approach to self-reporting and enhanced focus on the politics of reform could also help spur progress.

1.2.2. Progress in measuring support for fossil fuels in the context of the Sustainable Development Goals

The United Nations General Assembly adopted in July 2017 a global indicator framework to help monitor progress towards the 2030 Agenda for Sustainable Development. The agenda's 17 Sustainable Development Goals (SDGs) comprise 169 associated targets and 231 indicators (UN, 2020[71]). SDG 12, "ensure sustainable consumption and production patterns", includes a target to rationalise inefficient fossil-fuel subsidies that encourage wasteful consumption.[30] The target is tracked by SDG indicator 12.c.1, "Amount of fossil-fuel subsidies per unit of GDP (production and consumption)". UN Environment, the custodian agency for the indicator, released a methodology for measuring fossil-fuel subsidies in the context of the SDGs in June 2019, to help countries to report on the indicator and underpin measurement of support domestically and globally (UN Environment, OECD and IISD, 2019[72]) .

The methodology, "Measuring Fossil Fuel Subsidies in the Context of the Sustainable Development Goals", was developed with the OECD and the Global Subsidies Initiative (GSI) of the International Institute for Sustainable Development (IISD). It recommends a phased shift from using existing OECD, IEA and IMF global datasets to incorporating national figures as they become available (Figure 1.11), while recognising that reporting and monitoring capacity, and data availability, differ from country to country. Adopting the OECD Inventory approach, countries are invited to report disaggregated information on individual support measures, covering direct transfers and induced transfers (i.e. price regulation). Countries may also report on tax expenditures, other government revenue forgone and under-pricing of goods and services. Reporting on the final category of support is optional, given current data availability and the complexity of identifying and quantifying these support measures in a harmonised way.

Countries are nevertheless encouraged to start compiling these estimates and reporting existing information, in anticipation of a possible decision to fully integrate reporting on tax expenditures, other government revenue forgone and under-pricing of goods and services in 2025. Particularly for OECD member countries, which deliver the majority of support to fossil fuels through tax expenditures – or in some cases, all support (see Section 1.2.3) – tax expenditure data are intrinsic to a detailed understanding of overall support and therefore an accurate picture of progress towards the SDG indicator. The same can be said for at least the partner economies included in the Inventory, in which 43% of the total value of support is provided by tax expenditures. For the countries included, the Inventory is a significant tool that countries can use to identify and report on tax expenditures relevant to SDG indicator 12.c.1. The methodology developed by UN Environment, OECD and IISD acknowledges that more detailed, country-led guidance on measuring and monitoring support categories may also be required to integrate SDG indicator 12.c.1 reporting into national statistical systems, which could further support country reporting on tax expenditures.

Countries are additionally encouraged to provide data to assist in calculating the "price gap" where price regulation is in place, qualitative data on the scope of reported measures to provide context, and information on any reform efforts. Information on transfer of risk to government may be integrated into future national SDG monitoring, for example if a methodology for calculating such support is agreed internationally.

The national data collection process for SDG indicator 12.c.1 was anticipated to start at the end of 2020 with the launch of an "SDG 12 hub" web platform on the global SDG database website (UN, 2020[71]), but at publication the platform had yet to be launched. Data will be released in US dollars, as a percentage of GDP and on per capita. The proposal is to retain the OECD, IEA and IMF datasets as a complement to national figures even when country reporting is fully operational, to enhance comparability across economies.[31] The OECD is exploring with member countries how to ensure consistency between OECD Inventory figures (for which the primary country interlocutors are generally in ministries of finance) and national data on indicator 12.c.1 (to be reported by national statistical offices), including the possibility of the OECD playing an intermediary role in the SDG reporting process.

Figure 1.11. A stepwise approach to building a global SDG indicator 12.c.1 database centred on national reporting

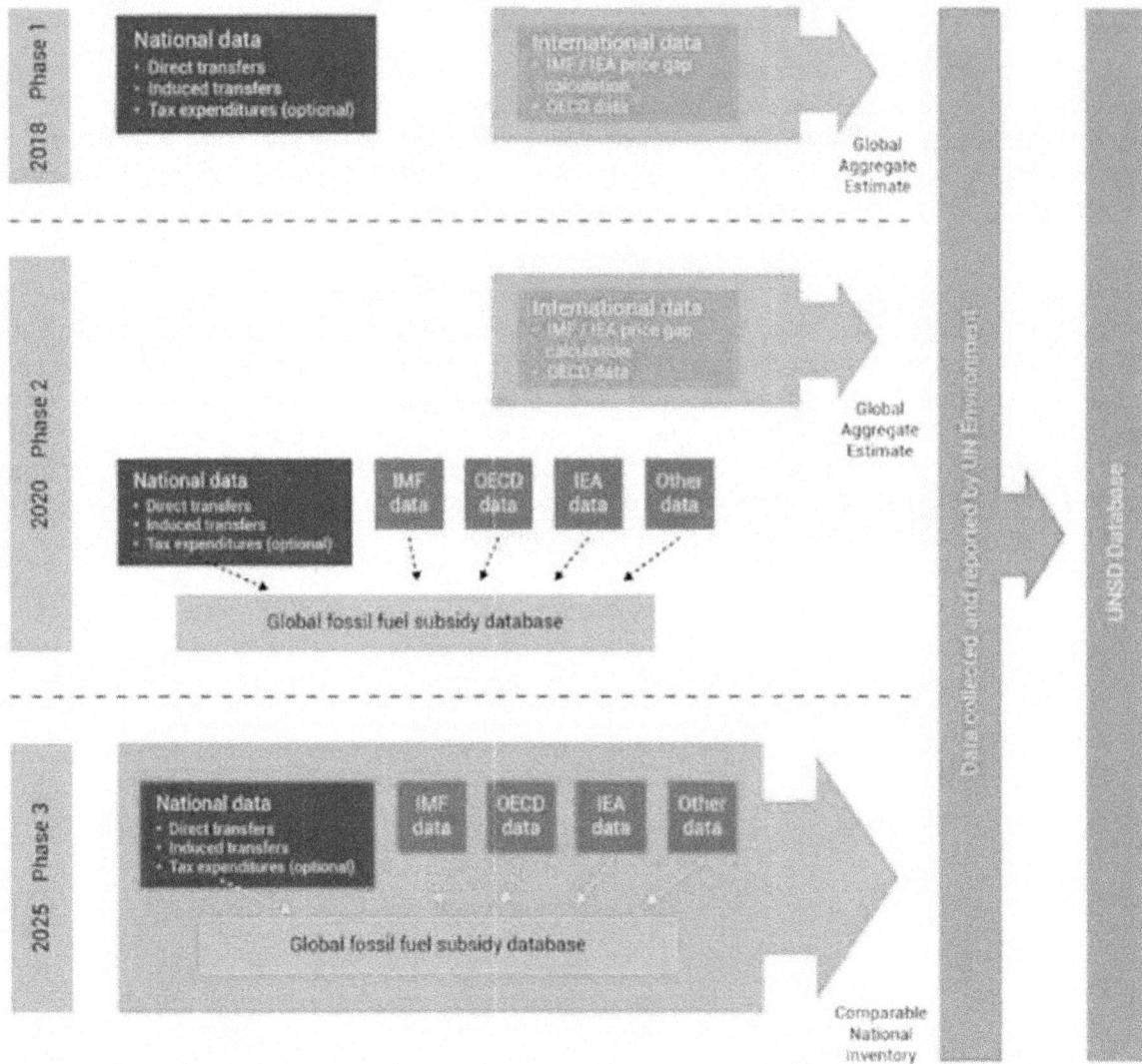

Source: (UN Environment, OECD and IISD, 2019[72])

1.2.3. Enhancing the interpretation of tax expenditure data

The 2015 Companion to the Inventory (OECD, 2015[3]) included significant discussion on how to understand tax expenditures relating to fossil fuels as documented in the Inventory. That discussion covered the types of tax expenditures, for example through lower rates, exemptions, or rebates for value-added taxes or excise taxes. It gave examples of more targeted tax expenditures, in the form of measures aimed at final consumption in favour of specific groups of consumers (e.g. preferential tax rates for residents of geographically or economically disadvantaged regions), specific types of fuels (e.g. lower tax rates or exemptions for diesel fuel used for transport, relative to gasoline), or related to how fuel is used (e.g. favourable tax rates for fuel use in primary industries). It also pointed to several caveats to bear in mind when interpreting Inventory tax expenditure data, or seeking to compare tax expenditure data across countries, particularly given that revenue forgone is generally calculated with reference to country-determined tax benchmarks (which also often differ between sectors and types of fuels).

Those caveats relate to both what is considered to be a tax expenditure – because there are different ways to set the benchmark tax treatment against which deviations are to be measured – and how to determine its size. Countries take different approaches to calculating tax expenditure estimates, and sometimes do not provide estimates of revenue forgone at all.[32] Countries might determine the benchmark regime through a conceptual assessment of "normal" taxation of income and consumption based on structural features of the tax system; by adopting a "reference-law approach" focused on expenditures that appear as such in law (e.g. tax credits, as opposed to differential tax treatment of two products); or based on tax reliefs squarely analogous to public spending (e.g. refundable income tax credits). In terms of calculating tax expenditures, the revenue-forgone method (rate of tax concession multiplied by base or uptake) is the most straightforward and common, but it is not universal. Different approaches to estimating tax expenditures associated with tax deferrals also cause valuations to differ (OECD, 2015[3]).

The range of possible approaches to defining country benchmarks, and the complexity of calculating tax expenditure data, can lead to higher estimates in several ways, affecting the international comparability of these data: higher benchmark tax rates; a more encompassing definition of the benchmark tax system, reflecting a greater number of measures; or simply more complete or up-to-date data, rather than higher levels of support. Nevertheless, country-defined benchmarks provide policy makers with considerable value as they allow the tracking of what countries themselves consider to be a tax expenditure measured as a deviation from their tax benchmark system. They also provide information on revenue that could be gained from policy reform.

The OECD has undertaken further work on how to improve the interpretation of tax expenditure data, prompted by exchanges with member countries on how to enhance the measurement and comparability of tax expenditure data and the prevalence of tax expenditures in the measures documented by the Inventory. OECD member countries deliver the bulk of their support to fossil fuels through the tax code, accounting for 75% of both the estimated value of support and the number of support measures.[33] While partner economies generally favour direct budgetary transfers, tax expenditures provide 43% of the total value of partner-economy support (Figure 1.12). In some countries (e.g. Austria, Azerbaijan, Belarus, Czech Republic, Denmark, Estonia, Finland, Luxembourg, Portugal, Sweden and the United Kingdom), virtually all support amounts for 2019 documented in the Inventory are provided through tax expenditures (Figure 1.12). Overall, 63% of total measures documented in the Inventory are tax expenditures, representing 62% of total support by value.

Figure 1.12. Tax expenditures are the predominant support mechanism in the majority of Inventory countries

By contrast, the majority of support in partner economies is administered as direct budgetary transfers

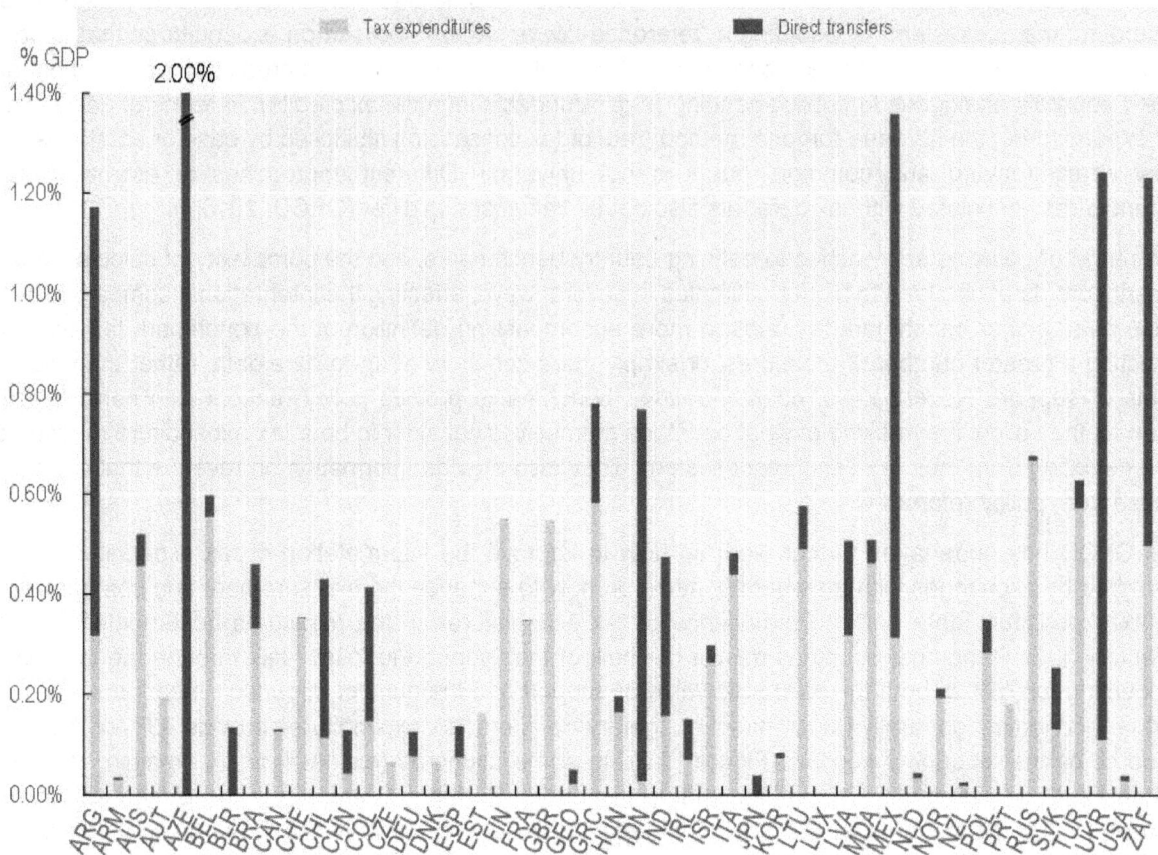

Note: Users of tax expenditure estimates should bear in mind that the Inventory records tax expenditures as estimates of revenue that is forgone due to a particular feature of the tax system that reduces or postpones tax relative to a jurisdiction's benchmark tax system, to the benefit of fossil fuels. Hence, (i) tax expenditure estimates could increase either because of greater concessions, relative to the benchmark tax treatment, or because of a rise in the benchmark itself; (ii) international comparison of tax expenditures could be misleading, due to country-specific benchmark tax treatments. Support estimate figures represent 2019 preliminary data.
Source: (OECD, 2020[11]); OECD National Accounts database (2020)

Analysis carried out by the OECD in 2019 that was shared with the OECD Joint Meeting of Tax and Environment Experts' country delegates revisited the 2015 Companion's discussion on the benefits and challenges in using tax expenditure estimates as a measure of fossil-fuel support. By casting the common benchmark for estimating tax expenditure data as the country-determined baseline tax code, the Inventory proposes an internationally comparable method for reporting revenue forgone through tax expenditures in support of fossil fuels, irrespective of the fact that a range of approaches can be adopted to determine and calculate those benchmarks. Nevertheless, limitations are imposed by the calculation of tax expenditure support data against country-specific benchmarks; their interpretation could be enhanced in several ways.

Enhancing interpretation of tax expenditure data to complement Inventory data and support national-level reporting on SDG Indicator 12.c.1

Using external benchmarks rather than domestic tax regime benchmarks is one way to improve interpretation of tax expenditure. Using an internationally agreed reference carbon price is one option to help overcome heterogeneous domestic benchmarks on fuel taxation (i.e. consumption-related tax expenditure data). Adopting a climate cost benchmark is in line with the approach adopted in the OECD work streams *Taxing Energy Use* (OECD, 2019[57]) and *Effective Carbon Rates* (OECD, 2018[73]), which compare effective tax and carbon rates against a low-end estimate of the climate costs of CO_2 emissions from fuel combustion (EUR 30 per tonne of CO_2) (USD 35.7),[34] thereby facilitating comparability across countries.

A 2019 OECD study focusing on the use of revenues from carbon taxes looked at how shifting from country benchmark tax rates to an external benchmark can aid international comparability of forgone revenue calculations (or revenue potential from carbon pricing) (Marten and van Dender, 2019[74]). The 2019 study proposes two benchmarks, including the EUR 30/tCO_2 low end estimate of the social cost of carbon.[35] It sets out actual and potential revenue from carbon pricing instruments as against this benchmark and as a share of GDP for the countries considered (Figure 1.13).

The study estimates carbon pricing revenue forgone from taxes and auction permits based on the gap between current prices and that benchmark to exceed actual revenues by 1.12 % as a share of GDP across OECD and G20 countries. That represents a low-end figure, as based on a conservative estimate of the social cost of emissions. In OECD member countries, the revenue forgone is estimated at 0.72% to 0.88% of revenue, basically equivalent to current revenues. This revenue can be interpreted as a form of revenue use "earmarked to apply a preferential effective carbon rate... to some or all emitters" when compared with the benchmark, with corresponding negative impacts on the effectiveness and cost-effectiveness of pricing measures (i.e. by reducing prices for some emitters and introducing heterogeneity into prices) (Marten and van Dender, 2019[74]).

Figure 1.13. Actual and potential revenues from carbon pricing instruments, EUR 30t/CO_2 benchmark, as a share of GDP (%)

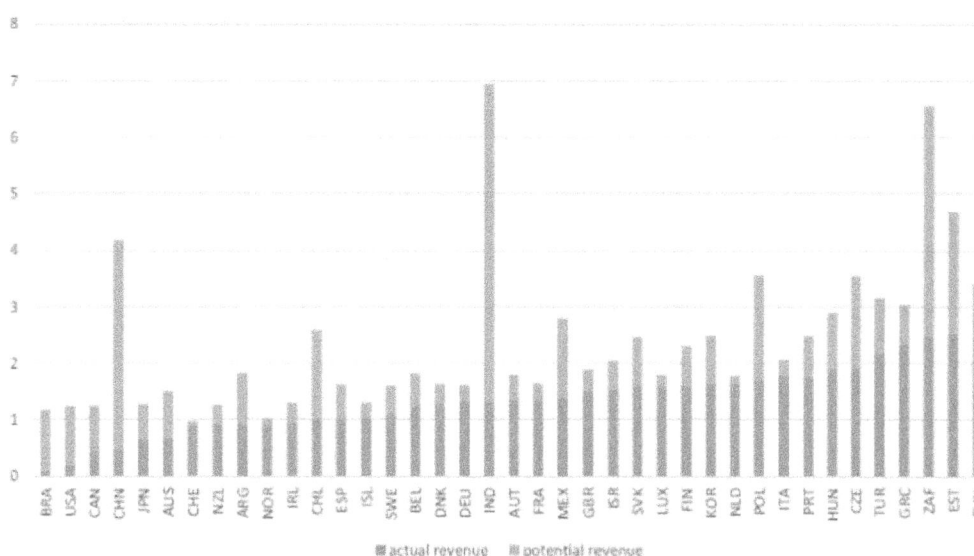

Note: Actual revenue estimates are based on the sum of energy taxes, carbon taxes and emissions trading system auction proceeds, see Annex A of (Marten and van Dender, 2019[74]) for the taxes included. Potential revenue estimates are based on (OECD, 2016[75]).
Source: (Marten and van Dender, 2019[74])

An important caveat to the use of a reference carbon price is that in economies where the existing effective carbon rate is higher than the benchmark rate, some instruments will go unaccounted for. In addition, when using an external as opposed to a domestic benchmark tax rate, the resulting calculation of revenue loss speaks less to countries' own contexts. The Swedish government, together with an expert sub-group of the London group on environmental accounts, is looking at how effective carbon price analysis might complement national tax reference rates and facilitate country comparisons in monitoring SDG indicator 12.c.1, including through the use of multiple, broadly defined tax bands (Steinbach, Palm and Byambakhorloo, 2020[76]). This would enable identification of negative effective carbon rates (i.e. due to support for fossil fuels), ranging up to maximum observed rates.[36] The Irish Central Statistical Office has set out calculations of fossil-fuel subsidies from 2000 to 2018 using average effective carbon rates for various fuels to facilitate assessment of forgone revenue against "reference" carbon prices (CSO, 2020[77]).

The 2019 OECD analysis on measurement and interpretation of fossil-fuel support through tax expenditures outlines two further options to enhance the interpretation and comparability of estimates of tax expenditures. The first is growth decomposition analysis to help assess different drivers of change in support over time, and specifically whether changes in support arise from explicit reform or simply structural changes to the underlying domestic benchmark tax regime. The second is effective tax rate analysis for production of fossil fuels (i.e. corporate effective rates), to inform on the extent to which tax expenditures provide investment incentives in upstream fossil-fuel industry segments.

Decomposing time trends in tax policies would require separating support estimates into benchmark tax rates and those applied to quantify revenue forgone, to isolate changes to underlying benchmark regimes. The growth rate in overall support estimates could be expressed as the sum total of changes in tax rates, fuel consumption, fuel prices, exchange rates and budgetary transfers, to enable a richer analysis of trends in support. In terms of accounting for the joint impact of the benchmark corporate income tax system and tax expenditures on upstream investment, effective tax rate analysis could help assess how both factors affect the "user cost of capital" for fossil-fuel producers, to infer the impact of fossil-fuel support (see Chapter 2). The OECD is considering further work in these areas to complement Inventory data and future national efforts to report on SDG Indicator 12.c.1.

References

Adomaitis, N. and T. Solsvik (2020), "Norway parliament grants more tax relief to oil sector", *Reuters*, https://www.reuters.com/article/us-health-coronavirus-norway-oil-idUSKBN23F1NV (accessed on 12 January 2021). [42]

Al Arabiya (2020), "Tunisia cuts fuel prices for the third consecutive month", *Al Arabiya*, https://english.alarabiya.net/en/business/energy/2020/06/08/Tunisia-cuts-fuel-prices-for-the-third-consecutive-month (accessed on 11 January 2021). [27]

Bala-Gbogbo, E. (2020), "Oil Crash Spurs Nigeria to End Fuel Subsidies, Risk Backlash", *Bloomberg*, https://www.bloomberg.com/news/articles/2020-05-09/oil-crash-spurs-nigeria-to-end-fuel-subsidies-risk-backlash (accessed on 11 January 2021). [25]

Banque de France (2020), *Communiqué: G20 Finance Ministers and Central Bank Governors Meeting 15 April 2020 [Virtual]*, https://www.banque-france.fr/sites/default/files/media/2020/04/17/g20_finance_ministers_and_central_bank_governors_meeting_communique_15_april_2020_final.pdf (accessed on 12 January 2021). [79]

Belchior, B., L. Duarte and B. Leite (2020), "Brazil: CNPE Publishes Resolution on Royalty Reduction for Fields Awarded to Small or Medium-Sized Companies", *Mayer Brown*, https://www.mayerbrown.com/en/perspectives-events/publications/2020/07/brazil-cnpe-publishes-resolution-on-royalty-reduction-for-fields-awarded-to-small-or-medium-sized-companies (accessed on 12 January 2021). [34]

Brown, M. (2020), "Trump administration cuts royalty rates for oil and gas", *AP News*, https://apnews.com/article/c82c1b9fefcfe083c8d29a7ecd65cc22 (accessed on 12 January 2021). [43]

Buckle, S. et al. (2020), "Addressing the COVID-19 and climate crises: Potential economic recovery pathways and their implications for climate change mitigation, NDCs and broader socio-economic goals", *OECD/IEA Climate Change Expert Group Papers*, No. 2020/04, OECD Publishing, Paris, https://dx.doi.org/10.1787/50abd39c-en. [80]

Cantillo, P. (2020), "Aislamiento dispara subsidio a la electricidad; aumenta 63% respecto a 2019", *Excelsior*, https://www.excelsior.com.mx/nacional/aislamiento-dispara-subsidio-a-la-electricidad-aumenta-63-respecto-a-2019/1393602/ (accessed on 11 January 2021). [22]

CGTN (2020), "Spain closes half its coal-fired power stations", *CGTN*, https://news.cgtn.com/news/2020-07-01/Spain-closes-half-its-coal-fired-power-stations-RLmZCviec0/index.html (accessed on 1 December 2020). [8]

CSO (2020), *Fossil Fuel Subsidies: CSO statistical release*, Central Statistics Office Ireland, https://www.cso.ie/en/releasesandpublications/er/ffes/fossilfuelsubsidies2018/ (accessed on 14 January 2021). [77]

Diamante, S. (2020), "Luz y gas. No habrá aumentos de tarifas hasta fin de año", *La Nación*, https://www.lanacion.com.ar/economia/oficial-el-gobierno-extendio-congelamiento-tarifas-180-nid2382449 (accessed on 11 January 2021). [19]

Dlouhy, J. (2020), "'Stealth Bailout' Shovels Millions of Dollars to Oil Companies", *Bloomberg*, https://www.bloomberg.com/news/articles/2020-05-15/-stealth-bailout-shovels-millions-of-dollars-to-oil-companies (accessed on 12 January 2021). [48]

Duranona, A. et al. (2019), "Argentina: National Executive Modifies Crude Oil and Fuel Price Freezing Scheme", *Baker McKenzie*, https://www.bakermckenzie.com/en/insight/publications/2019/09/national-executive-modifies-price-freezing-scheme (accessed on 11 January 2021). [18]

Elgouacem, A. and P. Journeay-Kaler (2020), *The Netherlands's Effort to Phase Out and Rationalise its Fossil-Fuel Subsidies*, OECD/IEA, http://www.oecd.org/fossil-fuels/publication/2020-OECD-IEA-review-of-fossil-fuel-subsidies-in-the-Netherlands.pdf (accessed on 14 January 2021). [70]

Energy Policy Tracker (2020), *Methodology*, Energy Policy Tracker, https://www.energypolicytracker.org/methodology/ (accessed on 12 January 2021). [49]

European Commission (2019), "Evaluation of the Council Directive 2003/96/EC of 27 October 2003 restructuring the Community framework for the taxation of energy products and electricity", *SWD(2019)*, No. 329, European Commission, Brussels, https://ec.europa.eu/taxation_customs/sites/taxation/files/energy-tax-report-2019.pdf (accessed on 12 January 2021). [58]

France 24 (2019), "Iran radically raises petrol prices by 50 percent", *France 24*, https://www.france24.com/en/20191115-iran-radically-raises-petrol-prices-by-50-percent (accessed on 11 January 2021). [15]

G20 (2020), *G20 Riyadh Leaders' Declaration*, G20, Riyadh, http://www.g20.utoronto.ca/2020/2020-g20-leaders-declaration-1121.html (accessed on 12 January 2021). [60]

G20 (2018), *G20 Energy Ministers Communiqué*, G20, Bariloche, http://www.g20.utoronto.ca/2018/2018-06-15-energy_communique.html (accessed on 12 January 2021). [62]

G20 (2013), *G20 Leaders' Declaration*, G20, Saint Petersburg, http://www.g20.utoronto.ca/2013/2013-0906-declaration.html (accessed on 12 January 2021). [61]

Gilbert, J. (2020), "Biggest Shale Play Outside of Texas Gets $5.1 Billion Lifeline", *Bloomberg*, https://www.bloomberg.com/news/articles/2020-10-22/biggest-shale-play-outside-of-texas-gets-5-1-billion-lifeline (accessed on 12 January 2021). [33]

Gould, T., Z. Adam and M. Walton (2020), "Low fuel prices provide a historic opportunity to phase out fossil fuel consumption subsidies", *International Energy Agency*, https://www.iea.org/articles/low-fuel-prices-provide-a-historic-opportunity-to-phase-out-fossil-fuel-consumption-subsidies (accessed on 11 January 2021). [13]

Government of Canada (2021), *Canada's COVID-19 Economic Response Plan*, Government of Canada, https://www.canada.ca/en/department-finance/economic-response-plan.html#energy (accessed on 12 January 2021). [37]

Government of Canada (2020), *Indigenous Natural Resource Partnerships*, Government of Canada, https://www.nrcan.gc.ca/our-natural-resources/indigenous-natural-resources/indigenous-natural-resource-partnerships/22197 (accessed on 12 January 2021). [36]

IDN Financials (2020), "Government drafts US$8.6 billion bailout for state-owned enterprises", *IDN Financials*, https://www.idnfinancials.com/news/34321/government-drafts-us-bailout-state-owned-enterprises (accessed on 12 January 2021). [38]

IEA (2020), *Kazakhstan energy profile*, International Energy Agency, Paris, https://www.iea.org/reports/kazakhstan-energy-profile#abstract (accessed on 11 January 2021). [16]

IEA (2020), *Key World Energy Statistics 2020*, International Energy Agency, Paris, https://www.petrolfed.be/sites/default/files/editor/Key_World_Energy_Statistics_2020_0.pdf (accessed on 12 January 2021). [56]

IEA (2020), "Low fuel prices provide a historic opportunity to phase out fossil fuel consumption subsidies", *International Energy Agency*, https://www.iea.org/articles/low-fuel-prices-provide-a-historic-opportunity-to-phase-out-fossil-fuel-consumption-subsidies (accessed on 11 January 2021). [23]

IEA (2020), *World Energy Balances (Database)*, https://www.iea.org/subscribe-to-data-services/world-energy-balances-and-statistics (accessed on 1 December 2020). [10]

IEA (2020), *World Energy Outlook 2020*, OECD Publishing, Paris, https://dx.doi.org/10.1787/557a761b-en. [24]

Lee, G. (2019), "ESB to close two peat-fired Midlands power stations", *RTE*, https://www.rte.ie/news/2019/1108/1089500-esb-power-plants/ (accessed on 1 December 2020). [5]

Lefebvre, B. (2020), "Trump administration cuts royalty payments for oil companies", *Politico*, https://www.politico.com/news/2020/05/21/trump-administration-cuts-royalty-payments-for-oil-companies-273548 (accessed on 12 January 2021). [45]

Lewis, A. and A. Elumami (2019), "Libyan gov't raises commercial price for kerosene as first step in reforms", *Reuters*, https://www.reuters.com/article/libya-energy-idUKL5N2716D2?edition-redirect=uk (accessed on 11 January 2021). [17]

Mander, B. (2020), "Argentina plans to set $45 oil price in push to save Vaca Muerta", *Financial Times*, https://www.ft.com/content/e76563f0-1fe3-4f95-8372-8ac1c970bcd4 (accessed on 12 January 2021). [31]

Marten, M. and K. van Dender (2019), "The use of revenues from carbon pricing", *OECD Taxation Working Papers*, No. 43, OECD Publishing, Paris, https://dx.doi.org/10.1787/3cb265e4-en. [74]

Matheson, T. (2020), "Who Benefits From The CARES Act Tax Cuts?", *Tax Policy Center, Urban Institute & Brookings Institution*, https://www.taxpolicycenter.org/taxvox/who-benefits-cares-act-tax-cuts (accessed on 12 January 2021). [47]

Meyer, G. (2020), "Oil groups boosted by cuts to US royalty rates during pandemic", *Financial Times*, https://www.ft.com/content/4d3d88c8-7eb6-4d06-bec0-c0ca8d91a045 (accessed on 12 January 2021). [44]

Middle East Monitor (2019), "Egypt cuts fuel subsidies by 40.5%, electricity by 75%", *Middle East Monitor*, https://www.middleeastmonitor.com/20190417-egypt-cuts-fuel-subsidies-by-40-5-electricity-by-75/ (accessed on 11 January 2021). [14]

OECD (2021), *Coronavirus - Data insights*, OECD, http://www.oecd.org/coronavirus/en/data-insights/ (accessed on 12 January 2021). [52]

OECD (2021), *EaP GREEN: Greening economies in the European Union's Eastern Partnership countries*, OECD, http://www.oecd.org/environment/eapgreen.htm (accessed on 14 January 2021). [82]

OECD (2021), *Focus on green recovery*, OECD, http://www.oecd.org/coronavirus/en/themes/green-recovery (accessed on 12 January 2021). [51]

OECD (2020), "Building back better: A sustainable, resilient recovery after COVID-19", *OECD Policy Responses to Coronavirus (COVID-19)*, http://www.oecd.org/coronavirus/policy-responses/building-back-better-a-sustainable-resilient-recovery-after-covid-19-52b869f5/ (accessed on 11 January 2021). [30]

OECD (2020), "COVID-19 and the low-carbon transition: Impacts and possible policy responses", *OECD Policy Responses to Coronavirus (COVID-19)*, http://www.oecd.org/coronavirus/policy-responses/covid-19-and-the-low-carbon-transition-impacts-and-possible-policy-responses-749738fc/ (accessed on 12 January 2021). [53]

OECD (2020), *Environment Database - Sustainable Ocean Economy*, OECD, https://stats.oecd.org/index.aspx?datasetcode=OCEAN (accessed on 12 January 2021). [59]

OECD (2020), "Environmental health and strengthening resilience to pandemics", *OECD Policy Responses to Coronavirus (COVID-19)*, http://www.oecd.org/coronavirus/policy-responses/environmental-health-and-strengthening-resilience-to-pandemics-73784e04/ (accessed on 12 January 2021). [50]

OECD (2020), *From containment to recovery: Environmental responses to the COVID-19 pandemic*, OECD, http://www.oecd.org/coronavirus/policy-responses/from-containment-to-recovery-environmental-responses-to-the-covid-19-pandemic-92c49c5c/ (accessed on 12 January 2021). [54]

OECD (2020), "Making the green recovery work for jobs, income and growth", *OECD Policy Responses to Coronavirus (COVID-19)*, http://www.oecd.org/coronavirus/policy-responses/making-the-green-recovery-work-for-jobs-income-and-growth-a505f3e7/ (accessed on 11 January 2021). [29]

OECD (2020), *OECD Inventory of Support Measures for Fossil Fuels (database)*, https://www.oecd.org/fossil-fuels/data/. [1]

OECD (2019), *Indonesia's effort to phase out and rationalise its fossil-fuel subsidies: A report on the G20 peer-review of inefficient fossil-fuel subsidies that encourage wasteful consumption in Indonesia*, OECD, https://www.oecd.org/fossil-fuels/publication/G20%20peer%20review%20Indonesia_Final-v2.pdf (accessed on 11 January 2021). [21]

OECD (2019), *Taxing Energy Use 2019: Using Taxes for Climate Action*, OECD Publishing, Paris, https://dx.doi.org/10.1787/058ca239-en. [57]

OECD (2018), *Effective Carbon Rates 2018: Pricing Carbon Emissions Through Taxes and Emissions Trading*, OECD Publishing, Paris, https://dx.doi.org/10.1787/9789264305304-en. [73]

OECD (2018), *Inventory of Energy Subsidies in the EU's Eastern Partnership Countries*, Green Finance and Investment, OECD Publishing, Paris, https://dx.doi.org/10.1787/9789264284319-en. [78]

OECD (2018), *OECD Companion to the Inventory of Support Measures for Fossil Fuels 2018*, OECD Publishing, Paris, https://dx.doi.org/10.1787/9789264286061-en. [2]

OECD (2016), *Effective Carbon Rates: Pricing CO2 through Taxes and Emissions Trading Systems*, OECD Publishing, Paris, https://dx.doi.org/10.1787/9789264260115-en. [75]

OECD (2015), *OECD Companion to the Inventory of Support Measures for Fossil Fuels 2015*, OECD Publishing, Paris, https://dx.doi.org/10.1787/9789264239616-en. [3]

OECD/IEA (2019), *Update on recent progress in reform of inefficient fossil-fuel subsidies that encourage wasteful consumption*, http://www.oecd.org/fossil-fuels/publication/OECD-IEA-G20-Fossil-Fuel-Subsidies-Reform-Update-2019.pdf (accessed on 11 March 2020). [11]

OECD and IEA (2019), *Update on Recent Progress in Reform of Inefficient Fossil-Fuel Subsidies that Encourage Wasteful Consumption*, G20, Toyama, http://www.oecd.org/fossil-fuels/publication/OECD-IEA-G20-Fossil-Fuel-Subsidies-Reform-Update-2019.pdf (accessed on 12 January 2021). [63]

Pandey, D. (2019), "CAG sees diversion of LPG cylinders for commercial use", *The Hindu*, https://www.thehindu.com/news/national/ujjwala-scheme-cag-suspects-huge-diversion-of-cylinders-for-commercial-use/article30284942.ece (accessed on 11 January 2021). [20]

Petkova, N. (2021), *Fossil-Fuel Subsidies in the EU's Eastern Partnership Countries: Estimates and Recent Policy Developments*, OECD, Paris. [81]

PPCA (2021), *PPCA Members*, https://poweringpastcoal.org/members (accessed on 1 December 2020). [9]

Presidência da República (2020), "Nº 31, de 15 de junho de 2020. Resolução nº 4, de 4 de junho de 2020, do Conselho Nacional de Política Energética - CNPE. Aprovo. Em 30 de junho de 2020.", *Diário Oficial da União*, https://www.in.gov.br/en/web/dou/-/despacho-do-presidente-da-republica-264424998 (accessed on 12 January 2021). [35]

Rystad Energy (2020), "Tax Relief Lowers Breakeven Prices For Norwegian Oil Drillers", *Rystad Energy*, https://oilprice.com/Energy/Energy-General/Tax-Relief-Lowers-Breakeven-Prices-For-Norwegian-Oil-Drillers.html (accessed on 12 January 2021). [41]

S&P Global Platts (2020), "Mexico cuts taxes for Pemex to help it cope with crisis", *S&P Global Platts*, https://www.spglobal.com/marketintelligence/en/news-insights/latest-news-headlines/mexico-cuts-taxes-for-pemex-to-help-it-cope-with-crisis-57929706 (accessed on 12 January 2021). [40]

Steenblik, R. et al. (2019), *Italy's effort to phase out and rationalise its fossil-fuel subsidies: A report on the G20 peer-review of inefficient fossil-fuel subsidies that encourage wasteful consumption in Italy*, G20, https://www.oecd.org/fossil-fuels/publication/Italy%20G20%20Peer%20Review%20IFFS%20.pdf (accessed on 14 January 2021). [67]

Steenblik, R. and M. Mateo (2020), "Western Europe's Long Retreat from Coal and Implications for Energy Trade", *World Trade Review*, Vol. 19/S1, pp. s98-s119, http://dx.doi.org/10.1017/s1474745620000269. [7]

Steenblik, R. et al. (2017), *Germany's effort to phase out and rationalise its fossil-fuel subsidies: A report on the G20 peer-review of inefficient fossil-fuel subsidies that encourage wasteful consumption in Germany*, G20, https://www.oecd.org/fossil-fuels/Germany-Peer-Review.pdf (accessed on 14 January 2021). [64]

Steenblik, R. et al. (2016), *The United States' efforts to phase out and rationalise its inefficient fossil-fuel subsidies A report on the G20 peer review of inefficient fossil-fuel subsidies that encourage wasteful consumption in the United States*, G20, http://www.oecd.org/fossil-fuels/publication/United%20States%20Peer%20review_G20_FFS_Review_final_of_2016090 2.pdf (accessed on 14 January 2021). [68]

Steenblik, R. et al. (2016), *China's efforts to phase out and rationalise its inefficient fossil-fuel subsidies: A report on the G20 peer review of inefficient fossil-fuel subsidies that encourage wasteful consumption in China*, G20, https://www.oecd.org/fossil-fuels/publication/G20%20China%20Peer%20Review_G20_FFS_Review_final_of_20160902. pdf (accessed on 14 January 2021). [66]

Steenblik, R. et al. (2017), *Mexico's efforts to phase out and rationalise its fossilfuel subsidies: A report on the G20 peer-review of inefficient fossil-fuel subsidies that encourage wasteful consumption in Mexico*, G20, https://www.oecd.org/fossil-fuels/Mexico-Peer-Review.pdf (accessed on 14 January 2021). [65]

Steinbach, N., V. Palm and A. Byambakhorloo (2020), *Monitoring greenhouse gas transfers: Focusing on transfers related to fossil fuel for monitoring Agenda 2030 and SEEA*, Statistics Sweden, Environment and Regions, https://www.scb.se/contentassets/f6eddbfd7acf43e7a486056912d50b5e/mi1301_2018a01_br _mi71br2001.pdf (accessed on 14 January 2021). [76]

Suharsono, A. and L. Lontoh (2020), *Indonesia's Energy Policy Briefing*, IISD-GSI, https://www.iisd.org/system/files/2020-08/indonesia-energy-policy-briefing-july-2020-en.pdf (accessed on 11 January 2021). [28]

Suzuki, J. and T. Nakano (2018), "Indonesia's Widodo backtracks on fuel aid as elections near", *Nikkei Asia*, https://asia.nikkei.com/Politics/Indonesia-s-Widodo-backtracks-on-fuel-aid-as-elections-near (accessed on 14 January 2021). [69]

The Associated Press (2018), "Germany Closes Its Last Black Coal Mine", *The New York Times*, https://www.nytimes.com/2018/12/24/business/germany-closes-its-last-black-coal-mine.html (accessed on 1 December 2020). [6]

U.S. DOE (2020), "DOE Announces Intent to Provide $122M to Establish Coal Products Innovation Centers", *U.S. Department of Energy*, https://www.energy.gov/articles/doe-announces-intent-provide-122m-establish-coal-products-innovation-centers (accessed on 12 January 2021). [46]

UN (2021), *SDG 12: Ensure sustainable consumption and production patterns*, United Nations, https://sdgs.un.org/goals/goal12 (accessed on 14 January 2021). [83]

UN (2020), *Global SDG Indicators Database*, United Nations, https://unstats.un.org/sdgs/indicators/database/ (accessed on 14 January 2021). [71]

UN (2020), *The Sustainable Development Goals Report*, United Nations Department of
Economic and Social Affairs, New York, https://unstats.un.org/sdgs/report/2020/The-
Sustainable-Development-Goals-Report-2020.pdf (accessed on 12 January 2021).

[55]

UN Environment, OECD and IISD (2019), *Measuring fossil fuel subsidies in the context of the
sustainable development goals*, UN Environment, Nairobi, Kenya,
https://wedocs.unep.org/bitstream/handle/20.500.11822/28111/FossilFuel.pdf?sequence=1&i
sAllowed=y (accessed on 23 September 2019).

[72]

Webber, J. (2020), "Mexico's Pemex: from cash cow to resource drain", *Financial Times*,
https://www.ft.com/content/4958eef9-7ce7-41c1-b2ff-8ea30ab0082b (accessed on
12 January 2021).

[39]

Webber, J. (2019), "Mexico: López Obrador makes a big bet on oil", *Financial Times*,
https://www.ft.com/content/d5c3c1c0-e432-11e9-b112-9624ec9edc59 (accessed on
8 September 2020).

[4]

Wood Mackenzie (2020), "Argentina weighs new price subsidy, but freezes gas tariffs", *Wood
Mackenzie*, https://www.woodmac.com/press-releases/argentina_gas_market_policy_plan/
(accessed on 12 January 2021).

[32]

Wooders, P. and T. Moerenhout (2020), "How to raise an easy $1 billion per day for the COVID-
19 recovery", *IISD-GSI*, https://www.iisd.org/gsi/subsidy-watch-blog/fuel-tax-covid-19-
recovery (accessed on 11 January 2021).

[26]

Zizhu, Z. (2021), "Decision Time for China on Fishing Subsidies", *The Maritime Executive*,
https://www.maritime-executive.com/editorials/decision-time-for-china-on-fishing-subsidies
(accessed on 11 January 2021).

[12]

Notes

[1] A comprehensive discussion of the Inventory approach to estimating support for fossil fuels, including the database's structure, coverage, data collection processes and the conceptual framework used to transform and collate primary data, is included in the *OECD Companion to the Inventory of Support Measures for Fossil Fuels 2015* (OECD, 2015[3]). Section 1.2.3 provides an overview of how to understand tax expenditures related to fossil fuels as documented in the Inventory, including caveats to bear in mind when interpreting Inventory tax expenditure data.

[2] Costa Rica was not an OECD member at the time of preparation of this publication and not yet reflected in the Inventory. Accordingly, references to OECD member countries as a zone should be read to exclude Costa Rica.

[3] GSSE includes measures benefiting producers or consumers collectively, as well as measures that do not increase current production or consumption of fossil fuels but may do so in the future (e.g. support for industry-specific infrastructure development such as coal or natural gas terminals, or fossil fuel-focused R&D). This report uses 2017 as its reference year, to enable assessment of trends since publication of the previous Companion (OECD, 2018[2]).

[4] The prevalence of consumer support in OECD member countries predominantly reflects the fact that many large OECD economies are resource poor and do not extract fossil fuels at significant scale. For OECD member countries in which fossil fuels are relatively abundant, the share of producer support tends to be higher – 46% in Canada, for example, and 40% in Germany in 2019.

[5] The Public Service Obligation levy continues to support renewables.

[6] The OECD's tracking and estimating of government support for fossil fuel production and consumption have traditionally used "support" rather than subsidy. However, the two terms are used interchangeably in this publication.

[7] Norway and the United Kingdom are the only Western European countries still mining hard coal (Steenblik and Mateo, 2020[7])

[8] The predominance of crude oil and petroleum product support, as well as consumer support over producer support, is partly due to the large share of petroleum products in countries' total primary energy supply and the fact that transport fuels tend to be taxed more on average than other sources of energy (resulting in larger tax expenditures from tax concessions) (OECD, 2015[3]).

[9] See the *OECD Companion to the Inventory of Support Measures for Fossil Fuels 2018* for a full explanation of the IEA approach to estimating fossil fuel consumption subsidies and the methodology used to aggregate OECD and IEA estimates (OECD, 2018[2]). Together, the economies covered represented 91% of world energy supply in 2018.

[10] China ceased publishing official fuel subsidy data starting in 2011, so it has not been possible to document this shift via official sources, contrary to usual Inventory practice.

[11] In the long run, however, lower electricity prices may encourage residential users to adopt non-fossil technologies such as electric vehicles, or abandon more CO_2-intensive methods of heating or cooling.

[12] For example, measures giving preferential treatment to natural gas used for electricity production over other types of use (e.g. industrial, commercial or residential use of natural gas subjected to higher, market-level tariffs). Output-based support data have not previously been made available because it is difficult to isolate government support for end users of fossil fuel-based energy from broader electricity consumer support (see Annex Table A.1). In addition, trade in electricity can make it difficult to trace the origin and consequently, the generation type of electricity once it has joined a country's national grid.

[13] G20 finance ministers recognised this opportunity in committing to support "an environmentally sustainable and inclusive recovery" in April 2020 (Banque de France, 2020[79]). The OECD has provided analysis of different pathways open to governments to rekindle economic activity specifically in the climate context, prioritising rapid re-establishment of economic growth and macroeconomic stability ("Rebound"), restoration of economic growth and macroeconomic stability along with an absolute decoupling of CO2 emissions ("Decoupling") and an integrated approach to economic recovery, CO_2 emissions reductions and well-being outcomes ("Wider Well-Being") (Buckle et al., 2020[80]).

[14] The Energy Policy Tracker includes in the calculation of its estimates payment, fine and interest accrual moratoriums to both private and state-owned enterprises, and support to fossil-fuel consuming capital (e.g., airline bailouts, grants to airport administrators, docking fee exemptions for maritime companies) Both of these categories of support fall outside the OECD's definition of support for the purposes of the Inventory, so caution should be applied when comparing Inventory figures with Energy Policy Tracker aggregate estimates.

[15] To note that the Inventory captures such support to the extent that information enabling apportionment of the share of support to fossil fuel industries (i.e., isolating the support amounts received by fossil fuel industries among other industry beneficiaries through calculated shares) is available.

[16] The Inventory adopts the IEA World Energy Balances categorisation of fossil fuel production and consumption sectors. Annex Table A.2 describes the methodology used to allocate support among sectors and the difficulties of isolating sectoral support.

[17] In addition, OECD-wide, 23% of total primary energy supply goes to the transport sector – more than any other sector – suggesting that significant levels of support might be anticipated.

[18] Such forms of support, as well as support provided through the corporate and personal income tax system, are methodologically more difficult to link to domestic energy use.

[19] It also aligns Inventory coverage with long-standing OECD work to support improvement of environmental policies in Eastern European, Caucasus and Central Asian transition economies (OECD, 2021[82]).

[20] The OECD previously published a regional study of energy subsidies for EaP countries in 2018 based on 2010-15 data (OECD, 2018[78]).

[21] For a full discussion of trends and reform priorities in EaP countries, see (Petkova, 2021[81]), on which discussion in this section is based.

[22] The tagging exercise was completed prior to inclusion of the EaP countries in the Inventory and hence represents a lower-bound of Inventory measures potentially relevant to ocean sustainability, covering 42 of 50 countries only, with a total of 1 170 overall measures as documented in the 2019 edition of the Inventory.

[23] A detailed discussion of the tagging methodology used to identify ocean-relevant fossil fuel support measures can be found in Annex A.3. This section is based on a broader, internal OECD paper authored by colleague Ivan Haščič "Monitoring progress towards a Sustainable Ocean Economy", with further information available on the OECD's Environment at a Glance Indicators Sustainable ocean economy webpage.

[24] Including Cannes (2011), Los Cabos (2013), Saint Petersburg (2013), Brisbane (2014), Antalya (2015), Hangzhou (2016), Hamburg (2017) and Osaka (2019) summits.

[25] Australia, Brazil, the European Union, Japan, Republic of Korea, the Russian Federation, Saudi Arabia, South Africa, Turkey and the United Kingdom are yet to undertake a peer review or initiate the process.

[26] They are Peru (2014), New Zealand (2015), the Philippines (2015) and Chinese Taipei (2017) (OECD and IEA, 2019[63]). APEC activity on reform of inefficient fossil-fuel subsidies has stalled since 2017.

[27] As the peer reviews are voluntary, G20 countries may of course seek to adjust this process for subsequent reviews.

[28] The medium time horizon for the commitment similarly remains undefined.

[29] EU countries are required to report on actions taken to phase out fossil fuel subsidies under the EU Regulation on the Governance of the Energy Union and Climate Action.

[30] The full target 12.c is to "rationalise inefficient fossil-fuel subsidies that encourage wasteful consumption by removing market distortions, in accordance with national circumstances, including by restructuring taxation and phasing out those harmful subsidies, where they exist, to reflect their environmental impacts, taking fully into account the specific needs and conditions of developing countries and minimising the possible adverse impacts on their development in a manner that protects the poor and the affected communities" (UN, 2021[83]).

[31] I.e., IMF and IEA data on support for consumption of fossil fuels, and OECD Inventory data on direct transfers of funds and tax expenditures in support of both fossil fuel production and consumption.

[32] For the 2020 edition of the Inventory, of 1 329 measures identified, 301 had no data available. Of these 301 measures, 256 are tax expenditures. This highlights that the Inventory estimates represent a lower bound figure.

[33] Because larger tax expenditures will result from tax concessions if high nominal taxes on fossil fuels are in place, and lower tax expenditures if nominal rates are low, rates of tax have a strong bearing on levels of support administered through the tax system. See the discussion of the impact of high OECD country tax rates in the context of the transport sector specifically in Section 1.1.4.

[34] *Effective Carbon Rates* uses an additional midpoint estimate of the social cost of carbon of EUR 60 (USD 71) as a second benchmark rate. The forthcoming 2021 edition will additionally include a EUR 120 (USD 142) benchmark.

[35] The second is the median effective carbon rate among (non-zero) sector-level effective carbon rates across all countries.

[36] The OECD's forthcoming *Taxing Energy Use for Sustainable Development* will model such negative carbon prices.

2 Designing reform of support for fossil fuels: a methodology for a robust sequential approach in OECD and G20 countries

Chapter 2 proposes a methodology for a sequential approach to designing fossil-fuel subsidy reforms in OECD and G20 countries, to assist governments assess and address the effects of support measures and their reform, and spur enduring change. Sections 2.1 and 2.2 present the rationale for a sequential approach, and provide an overview of possible steps and associated tools. Section 2.3 considers how governments might identify support measures, document their objectives and estimate their budgetary cost, as a crucial first step towards reform. Section 2.4. addresses how to isolate measures that result in the most significant changes to economic decision-making and environmental performance across different segments of the fossil-fuel value chain, to establish priorities for reform. Section 2.5 identifies analytical tools to inform on possible economic and social effects of reform. Section 2.6 examines how reform measures may be accompanied by complementary policies to alleviate any negative effects of reforms and channel fiscal savings to more productive uses. The chapter concludes with a discussion of how the OECD can support governments in applying the sequential approach and possible forward work priorities.

2.1. Why a sequential approach to reform?

Progress towards achieving the international commitments that countries have taken in the G20, G7 and APEC forums to phase out support for fossil fuels has been mixed, as Chapter 1 demonstrates. However, the case for sharper global focus on reform of fossil-fuel support has been strengthened by mounting climate ambition, fiscal pressure resulting from the COVID-19-induced recession and increasingly vocal calls to "build back better" as governments devise and implement economy recovery packages. In addition, the need for reform has been underlined by evidence that energy sector support in response to the COVID-19 crisis has been weighted in favour of incumbent fossil-fuel industries.

Comprehensive guidance to support reform processes tailored to OECD and G20 countries' circumstances has not previously been developed, despite the challenge involved to unwind government support for fossil-fuel production and consumption. Previous OECD studies of the effects of fossil-fuel support and their reform have generated qualitative tools to guide users in identifying environmental benefits of reform. An early look at the implications of fossil-fuel support under the umbrella of environmentally harmful subsidies produced a checklist for determining the likelihood of environmental benefits from reform (OECD, 2005[1]). An integrated assessment framework was later introduced to map out the objectives, cost-effectiveness, and incidental and long-term consequences of reform (OECD, 2007[2]). This work was presented to the G7 as part of a report produced at the request of Italy to support discussions in the environment stream of its 2017 G7 Presidency (Jésus et al., 2017[3]).

To fill the gap in comprehensive guidance and encourage reform – including in the context of COVID-19 recovery packages – this chapter sets out a sequential approach.[1] It offers a toolkit for each step along the reform trajectory to help governments assess and address the effects of fossil-fuel support measures and their reform. This approach builds on the latest research and accommodates the diversity of tax systems across OECD and G20 countries, to help each government build the evidence base it needs for its specific national context and reform process. The tools recommended vary in their level of ambition, difficulty, and data and resource intensity. But being modular by construction, the sequential approach enables different steps to be undertaken in isolation as countries identify specific needs and as their capacity to conduct analysis becomes available.

Countries can scale up the breadth and depth of their analysis at their own pace. Unavailability of resources to complete any one step does not preclude policy makers from proposing and proceeding with a reform agenda. The sequential approach can be viewed as a comprehensive research programme with which to gauge the depth and breadth of any given evaluation process. It can also help assess gaps in the evidence base that could be a source of weakness in designing reform. Carrying out a full suite of assessments in designing reform measures should minimise the risk of political backlash and backsliding that too often accompanies reform.

2.2. Four steps to assess government support measures and their reform

The sequential approach to analysing government support measures proposes four steps of analysis with associated tools (Table 2.1). The tools vary in their level of ambition, difficulty, as well as data and resource intensity.

Table 2.1. Four steps and associated tools for a robust sequential fossil fuel subsidy reform process

	Step in sequential approach	Objective	Analytical tools	Availability of the tool
1	Identify support measures, document their objectives and estimate their budgetary cost.	Measure the cost to government of providing support for fossil fuels. Understand the objective and intended beneficiaries of support measures.	OECD taxonomy of support measures for fossil fuels OECD PSE-CSE accounting framework IEA "price gap" method for estimating consumer price support G20 and APEC peer review frameworks	OECD Inventory IEA subsidies database IMF (pre-tax price-gap estimates portion only) G20 peer reviews
2	Measure the distortiveness of support measures, including their economic, social and environmental effects.	Rank support measures by their level of distortiveness on fossil-fuel production, investment, consumption and CO_2 emissions.	Effective tax rates (effective marginal tax rates, effective average tax rates) Sectoral models: extraction model of oil and gas, and a two-sector model of energy-intensive and non-energy-intensive industries OECD Inventory beneficiaries' data by broad economic sector	A quantitative extraction model and sectoral model is to be developed in the OECD. IMF Fiscal Analysis of Resource Industries (FARI) mode Information on tax expenditures for energy inputs to be included in OECD *Taxing Energy Use* and *Effective Carbon Rates* publications. Harberger's triangle measurement of "deadweight loss" (i.e. non-optimal production) using supply and demand elasticity estimates are to be developed by the OECD.
3	Identify the winners and losers of fossil-fuel support reform processes.	Analyse the distributional impact and other potential adverse effects of reform of support for fossil fuels.	Micro-simulation models (based on household and firm surveys) CGE models	OECD micro-simulation model for energy taxes Commitment to Equity (CEQ) Institute assessment tool OECD ENV-Linkages, OECD METRO, UCL Energy Institute models
4	Evaluate alternative policies with better economic, environmental, fiscal or distributional outcomes	Identify policies that increase the efficiency and improve the distributional impact of government intervention.	Micro-simulation models (based on household and firm surveys) CGE models	OECD ENV-Linkages, OECD METRO, UCL Energy Institute models

Note: The list of analytical tools is not exhaustive. It sets out the mostly frequently used tools in this policy area and those utilised by the OECD.

Countries should heed the broader policy environment as they deploy these assessment tools. Policy interactions should not be neglected; complementarities and redundancies should be identified and addressed along the way. The proposed multi-step approach takes into account the complexity and challenges that confront policy makers seeking to implement reform. Potential distributional and competitiveness implications can act as deterrents to reform and may warrant accompanying compensatory measures. The differentiated effects of support measures may also mean that some will not be a priority for reform as they are important for achieving a government's social or investment objectives, with no viable alternatives. The widespread use of tax expenditures in OECD and G20 countries to provide preferential treatment to the use and production of fossil-fuel requires deployment of specific tools suitable for studying their role in influencing economic decisions and environmental outcomes along the fossil-fuel value chain, as integral to the effective design of reform packages in these countries.

Moreover, because energy plays such a central role in OECD and G20 countries, the economic, social and environmental effects of fossil-fuel support typically spread far beyond the energy sector and its consumers. Reform of fossil-fuel support therefore requires a whole-economy approach, with careful consideration of potential adverse effects. Reform should be conceived within a country's national development plans, especially for developing G20 countries. The cross-cutting nature of fossil-fuel support, compared with support to specific sectors like agriculture and fisheries, means that understanding its effects on economic decisions and environmental outcomes can be a daunting task.

Similarly, government efforts to respond to the COVID-19-induced recession, enhance fiscal discipline and increase climate ambition should be conceived as part of a broader policy landscape. Efforts to integrate environmental considerations in the budgeting process have multiplied over recent years, both internationally and at the country level. The Paris Collaborative on Green Budgeting (PCGB), launched at the One Planet Summit in 2017, is a multilateral initiative to institutionalise the tracking and evaluation of public expenditure to ensure it is better aligned with climate goals and other environmental goals. The more recently formed Coalition of Finance Ministers on Climate Action has lent further support to the PCGB, as it encourages countries to take climate change into account in their macroeconomic and fiscal and budgeting planning. In 2019, France, as a founding member of the PCGB, proposed a framework that would be used to deliver a green budget statement as an annex to the general budget, starting with the 2020 fiscal year. The first green budget statement was duly delivered in 2020. Ireland commenced green budgeting practices in 2019 and has identified, tagged and estimated climate-related expenditure for the 2019, 2020 and 2021 budgets. Climate-related expenditure is defined as any expenditure that promotes, in whole or in part and directly or indirectly, Ireland's transition to a low-carbon, climate-resilient and environmentally sustainable economy (OECD, 2021[4]). Such undertakings can improve governments' understanding of the short- and long-term implications of budgetary decisions on climate and other environmental outcomes.

Spending reviews are widely used as a budgeting tool in OECD member countries to improve spending efficiency and reprioritise expenditures to align them better with government policy and fiscal objectives (OECD, 2019[5]). Since direct budgetary transfers and tax expenditures in support of fossil fuels result in forgone revenue, they might be evaluated as part of a country's spending review. The Netherlands' use of spending reviews to effect important reforms can be viewed as good practice (Box 1). The scope, frequency and evaluation methods of spending reviews vary from one country to another. Some countries undertake annual reviews of spending programmes in a specific policy area, such as Denmark, Ireland and the Netherlands (Elgouacem and Journeay-Kaler, 2020[6]). Others carry out comprehensive policy reviews every few years, such as the United Kingdom and, again, Ireland. As fossil-fuel support is delivered through different policy instruments (i.e. both through – tax and non-tax measures – and with different policy objectives in mind, single reviews are less likely to result in a comprehensive evaluation of support than broader policy review mechanisms.

Box 1. Spending reviews in the Netherlands are helping drive reform of support for fossil fuels

Periodic evaluation has proven to be an important driver for policy reform in the Netherlands. As the budgetary process requires government spending schemes to be evaluated every four to seven years, ministries have the opportunity to review policies and reform those they deem no longer effective or relevant. Evaluations can be carried out for specific policy areas, through an impact assessment of an individual measure or a cost-benefit analysis.

In addition to policy reviews of individual schemes, the government carries out interdepartmental policy reviews (*interdepartementale beleidsonderzoeken* or IBOs). IBOs are forward-looking as they identify options for policy adjustments and, unlike the targeted policy reviews, they are not confined to a specific policy area as defined in the budget law. This allows them to address broader social problems. Some ministries can choose to combine an IBO with a policy review, in which case both backward-looking and forward-looking evaluations are undertaken.

An OECD/IEA review of efforts to phase out and rationalise support for fossil fuels in the Netherlands, presented to the Dutch parliament in September 2020, found that policy reviews had resulted in the elimination of several measures providing preferential tax treatment to specific fossil fuels or end users. The measures had been found to be ineffective in reaching their policy objectives (Elgouacem and Journeay-Kaler, 2020[6]). Nevertheless, the review recommended that the government consider broadening the scope of tax and non-tax measures addressed in policy reviews, to help the country achieve its climate targets. For example, it suggests that the government consider expanding the scope of a planned 2020 evaluation of energy taxation to cover "all those support measures that confer a benefit to the use and production of fossil fuels", to provide a more complete and informed view of the situation. The initial scope of the evaluation excluded several measures related to the upstream oil and gas sector – in some instances because they were subject to review in separate evaluation rounds – including measures falling under the purview of the EU Energy Taxation Directive, tax expenditures related to fuel excise duties, and compensation to certain companies for the indirect costs arising from the EU Emissions Trading System.

2.3. Identifying support measures, documenting their objectives and estimating their budgetary cost

Reporting individual support programmes and their associated fiscal costs is a crucial first step towards reforming support for fossil fuels. Government policies can benefit fossil fuels through four different transfer mechanisms:

1. Direct spending;
2. Tax expenditures and other forgone government revenue;
3. Induced transfers (e.g. through market price support that results in observed domestic energy prices lower than international reference prices);
4. Transfer of risk to the government.

These policies can target different parts of the fossil-fuel supply value chain, changing the cost structure for producers and the price for end users.

The OECD Inventory approach provides an organising framework for tracking a wide and comprehensive range of government support for fossil fuels.[2] In the Inventory, individual government policies are classified not only by how public resources are transferred to their beneficiaries but also by the formal incidence of the measures along the fossil-fuel value chain, i.e. whether they benefit producer output returns, enterprise income, cost of intermediate inputs, factors of production, or final consumer prices and incomes (OECD, 2015[7]).[3] International efforts to develop a methodology to help track the SDG indicator for phasing out inefficient fossil-fuel subsidies (SDG 12.c.1.) have adopted the OECD Inventory approach to estimating support for fossil fuels (UN Environment, OECD and IISD, 2019[8]).

The key to building an inventory of support measures is to start by creating a comprehensive list of government policies and programmes that could be providing preferential treatment or benefits to fossil-fuel consumers and producers using a transfer mechanism taxonomy. The OECD Inventory represents an excellent resource in this respect for the 50 economies it covers. The inventory can then be populated with the corresponding estimates using readily available information and internationally established methods. Where no budgetary estimates are available for measures, reporting is still beneficial as it enhances transparency on government policies and can serve as a basis for future improvements.

The most straightforward government programmes to identify are direct spending programmes. These are well documented, revised on a budget cycle, and subject to legislative and executive branch scrutiny. Tax expenditures, however, are underreported in many jurisdictions. Only 26 of the 44 OECD and G20 economies included in the OECD Inventory produce tax expenditure reports that record the revenue forgone from providing tax benefits. In addition, the scope of what constitutes a tax expenditure can be substantially different from one jurisdiction to another. Tax expenditures are not subjected to regular evaluation procedures and therefore they remain opaque; this is a main reason explaining the lack of estimates of tax expenditures, in contrast with budgetary programmes.

Nevertheless, tax expenditures as well as direct spending programmes are the more readily identifiable forms of government support for fossil fuels in OECD and G20 economies and thus should be a priority in the reform process.[4] The OECD Inventory focuses on government support provided through these mechanisms because data for other forms of support are generally much more difficult to obtain or technically arduous to calculate (see below). An inventory of budgetary transfers and tax expenditures, as the first building blocks towards mapping the policy landscape of support, helps to understand how governments use fiscal instruments to implement energy, social and economic development policies.

2.3.1. Estimating the cost of direct spending and tax expenditures

The level of difficulty in measuring government support varies across the different transfer mechanisms. It ranges from the ease of quantifying the cost of direct spending programmes, to the estimation of induced transfers due to government regulation and the revenue forgone from providing tax benefits, to quantifying the support element of transferring risk to the government through concessional finance or loan guarantees. The estimation of support measures other than direct spending hinges on measuring the difference between applied tax rates, regulated price, interest rate and realised equity return, and their reference counterparts. Among the OECD and G20 economies whose tax expenditures are reported in the Inventory, a third do not have estimates for the incurred revenue forgone.

Estimating the cost to government of preferential loans and loan guarantees is particularly complex.[5] Government support through the financial system remains underreported despite its scale and its potential for affecting the allocation of capital across sectors and technologies. Tracking the value of potential support associated with concessional loans or risk transfers comes with much more demanding data requirements, as they need to be measured at the project level. For example, there exists no official government reporting of concessional loans and below-market equity to fossil-fuel related projects, with the exception of the OECD Development Assistance Committee (DAC)-reported grant equivalent of overseas development assistance (ODA) flows (OECD, 2021[9]). (OECD, 2018[10]) proposes a method to overcome methodological difficulties and quantify the support element of government credit assistance, but the Inventory does not yet cover this type of support.

Given that they do not encompass financial support estimates, the USD 178 billion value of the more than 1 300 individual direct transfers, induced transfers and tax expenditures documented in the 2020 OECD Inventory, as well as the more global OECD-IEA estimate of government support for the production and consumption of fossil fuels discussed in Chapter 2 (USD 478 billion in 2019), should therefore be understood as lower-bound estimates.[6]

2.3.2. Understanding the rationale for government support measures

It is not enough to estimate the fiscal cost a government incurs through a support measure. Part of the stock-taking exercise is also to understand the objective of each measure and its intended beneficiaries. Such information is important to help assess the relevance of the measure and to identify alternative measures that could meet the same policy objectives in a more efficient, equitable and environment-friendly manner. Unlike direct budgetary transfers for which evaluation processes exist on a periodic basis to inform the effectiveness of different spending programmes in reaching their goals and beneficiaries, tax expenditures often go unassessed, with minimal to no adjustments to their original provisions during their lifetime.

The economic rationale for government intervention is often to correct for market failures, such as imperfect competition, public goods, externalities, incomplete markets or informational asymmetries. Additional arguments are made for government intervention particularly when market outcomes do not deliver socially equitable income distribution, even if Pareto efficient (i.e. resulting in optimal overall welfare). Therefore, it is important to identify which market failure or distributional motivations are behind support measures and consider alternatives that are more cost-effective and efficient in addressing these objectives.

Countries can engage in a self-review or peer-review process to identify, quantify and evaluate their support measures for fossil fuels. Several countries have pursued peer reviews under the auspices of the G20 and APEC as part of their commitment to phase out inefficient fossil-fuel subsidies that encourage wasteful consumption; the Netherlands recently completed a "G20-style" peer review (see Chapter 1). These peer reviews culminate in reports by a reviewing panel comprised of representatives from different countries, international organisations and non-governmental organisations. Peer reviews discuss the energy, economic and overall policy environment in the country, enumerate support measures, their objectives and their effectiveness, and propose reforms.

2.4. Measuring the effects of support measures for fossil fuels and prioritising them for reform

A review and inventory of government support measures for fossil fuels are useful starting points for analysing their economic, environmental and distributional implications, and alternative policies that could deliver the same policy outcomes. Identifying measures with the biggest effects on economic decision-making and environmental performance can orient reform efforts to prioritise the most economically and environmentally distortive measures. The following sections propose analytical frameworks to examine how government interventions affect different segments of the fossil-fuel value chain: from the upstream and midstream sectors (exploration and development, production, processing, refining and transportation) to industrial, commercial, transport and residential end users.

By changing the cost structure for upstream investments, lowering input costs for consuming industries and distorting relative prices for other end users, support for fossil fuels induces behavioural responses that modify economic, social, and environmental outcomes. Producer support measures encourage excessive development of resources and shore up carbon-intensive production processes. This locks in CO_2-intensive capital in sectors that might otherwise make different choices with a view to long-term competitiveness, and slows the uptake of less carbon-intensive technologies. Support to end users often leads to wasteful consumption since it brings end-user energy prices below cost recovery or market prices, or confers preferential treatment to a select group, with the lower prices sometimes extending outside their intended target beneficiaries. As a result, support for fossil fuels facilitates lock-in of emissions-intensive infrastructure and slows down the transition towards a greener economy. Distortions are defined in this chapter as economic or environmental outcomes that result from government support and deviate from a benchmark case with no support instruments. Decisions that are influenced by government policies targeting fossil fuels in the upstream and downstream sectors are examined first, followed by a discussion of distortions emanating from household behavioural responses.

2.4.1. Evaluating support to the upstream fossil-fuel sector: effective tax rate analysis

Countries use several forms of government support, including tax incentives, concessional finance or direct budgetary transfers, to attract domestic and foreign investment. Investments in the fossil-fuel extractive sector can be important drivers for economic growth but are generally inconsistent with countries' commitments to reduce carbon emissions to net zero by 2050. Government support to the upstream fossil-fuel sector can erode a government's ability to fund public services and investments of higher priority. As well as tilting the playing field towards fossil-fuel energy sources, support for fossil fuels can crowd out investments in other industries.

Thus far, policies to limit climate change and to rein in government expenditure on fossil fuels have generally focused on demand-side policy instruments that aim to reduce greenhouse gas emissions and fossil-fuel use. Little has been done to explore opportunities for supply-side policies, despite governments' plans to change energy markets to integrate less emitting sources. However, the increasing number of economies committing to achieve net-zero emissions by 2050 including the European Union, France, Japan, Korea and the United Kingdom, will force further action in this area. Several experts, have called upon policy makers to consider policies that restrict fossil-fuel supply as part of climate change mitigation policy packages (Green and Denniss, 2018[11]) (Piggot et al., 2018[12]) (Faehn et al., 2017[13]). Several countries have committed to cut fossil-fuel supply by phasing out coal power generation (including the signatories to the Powering Past Coal Alliance), close uncompetitive coal mines (via the EU Council decision 2010/787/EU and Spain's "Framework Plan for Coal Mines and Mining Communities 2013-2018") and halt new exploration for oil and gas (including Costa Rica, Denmark and New Zealand, and Canada via its moratorium on Arctic oil and gas work). Carbon Tracker is leading a consortium to develop a Global Registry of Fossil Fuels intended to bring together standardised and government-vetted data on fossil-fuel reserves, licensed resources, and historical and projected production, to provide a baseline of fuels "known, estimated and planned for extraction" and enable assessment of related lock-in of emissions (Herr, 2020[14]).

This section provides a method for quantifying the influence of tax incentives and support measures on investment decisions in the upstream fossil-fuel sector compared with a reference benchmark fiscal system, i.e. that applied to the broader economy not benefitting from preferential tax treatment (Box 2). Given the diversity in fiscal measures (including tax incentives and other support measures) used to raise revenue from the sector (Elgouacem et al., 2020[15]), a synthetic indicator is proposed, via analysis of effective tax rates (ETRs), which allows for comparison across different fiscal regimes in an international context. ETRs differ from statutory tax rates depending on the access firms have to various forms of preferential tax treatment. Larger gaps between effective and benchmark tax rates are a measure of distortion in the sense that uniform treatment under the benchmark system would be more efficient.

For producers of fossil fuels, the user cost of capital plays an important role in allocating their investments for exploration, development and production. It represents the marginal product of capital (or return) that a firm needs to earn to pay the return required by investors and the marginal tax on its income, and to offset depreciated capital. Analysing how the user cost of capital is affected by changes in a fiscal regime enables inference of the degree of distortiveness of fossil-fuel support. Building on the concept of user cost, the effective marginal tax rate (EMTR) exposes the extent to which a fiscal regime affects firms' user cost and therefore investment and production incentives. It represents the wedge between the pre-tax return and the post-tax return of capital as a share of the pre-tax return.

The EMTR can be used to study how fiscal regimes affect investments at the margin – investments for which the return on capital is just sufficient to cover economic cost of investment. Therefore, this indicator reveals the effect of the fiscal regime on investments related to projects that are already in place, rather than investment in new projects.

Box 2. Benchmark fiscal regimes for oil and gas extraction

The choice of a benchmark fiscal regime is essential for the evaluation of different government spending programmes. The benchmark is a fiscal regime against which to measure behavioural responses of producers to different government incentives.

From an economic efficiency perspective, a neutral fiscal regime – whereby investment decisions at the margin are not impacted by the prevailing fiscal regime – represents a useful benchmark. Under such a system, oil and gas producers are liable for taxes, a combination of corporate income tax (CIT) and a resource rent tax (RRT), levied on their net profits. For such a system to be neutral, this RRT is only levied once a project has recovered all its exploration and development expenditures and reached a minimum rate of return. At that point, the project pays a high marginal tax rate.

A neutral benchmark fiscal regime is considered to be symmetrical, i.e. its marginal tax rate on income is the same as its marginal tax reduction rate on all costs related to the different phases of production in the oil and gas sector. (Daubanes and Andrade de Sá, 2014[16]) and (Gaudet and Lasserre, 2015[17]) lay out the conditions under which an RRT is neutral vis-à-vis the firm's investment decisions. The economic efficiency of this profit-based tax might be compromised if the government, as the resource owner, has the objective of raising the requisite revenue to ensure that it is compensated for the opportunity cost it incurs from extracting an exhaustible resource. (Conrad, Hool and Nekipelov, 2018[18]) underline this divergence in incentives between the producer and the resource owner and propose that a royalty could capture the scarcity value of the resource.

The opportunity cost of depleting an exhaustible resource cannot be ignored when constructing a benchmark system as it characterises the economic trade-offs facing this sector and the welfare implications for intergenerational equity. It is therefore useful to show whether the government, as the resource owner, recovers the asset value of the *in situ* resource through its tax system to ensure that future generations are taken into account. In the same spirit, the opportunity cost of the environmental implications of production can also be integrated into a benchmark fiscal regime, to reflect the constraints facing producers.

An alternative and widely used approach to designate a benchmark fiscal regime is to take the prevailing corporate tax system as the benchmark against which to compare the fiscal regime applied to the fossil-fuel sector. Such a benchmark abstracts from the economic efficiency discussion of the fiscal system and focuses on the preferential tax system applied to the sector using the country-specific baseline.

EMTRs can account for most of the incentives granted to corporations, including those in the upstream fossil-fuel sectors. (McKenzie and Mintz, 2011[19]), for example, apply the method to measure the extent to which the fiscal regime encourages investments in Canada's upstream sector at the provincial level and find that on aggregate, oil and gas production in Canada is still discouraged by the overall fiscal regime (positive EMTR). But they find that exploration and development are benefiting from a negative EMTR, and that the fiscal regime provides more benefits than levies taxes on these activities. Their paper falls short of showing how the aggregate EMTR for the oil and gas industry in Canada compares with the EMTR in other sectors, to ascertain whether the prevailing fiscal regime for oil and gas confers a preference for investment in this sector relative to other sectors.

When measured against a benchmark fiscal system – or EMTRs facing other sectors – the EMTR can be used to quantify the magnitude of the distortion emanating from a specific fiscal design relative to others. One study, using available data in the United States on the cost of debt and equity financing, shows that it is straightforward to derive the cost of finance, (i.e. the required return for investors) for different sectors. Taking a ratio of the pre-tax and after-tax cost of finance only (a component of the user cost of capital) for each sector shows that different fiscal industries, through their choice of the mix of equity and debt financing, have substantially different tax costs of finance (Figure 2.1). Although it is not clear from this exercise why those industries have adopted different finance mixes, the result is that the tax cost of financing investment in oil and gas production and exploration is among the lowest in the sample of sectors.

Figure 2.1. The effect of taxation on the cost of raising funds through a combination of equity and debt in the United States differs substantially from one sector to another (2018)

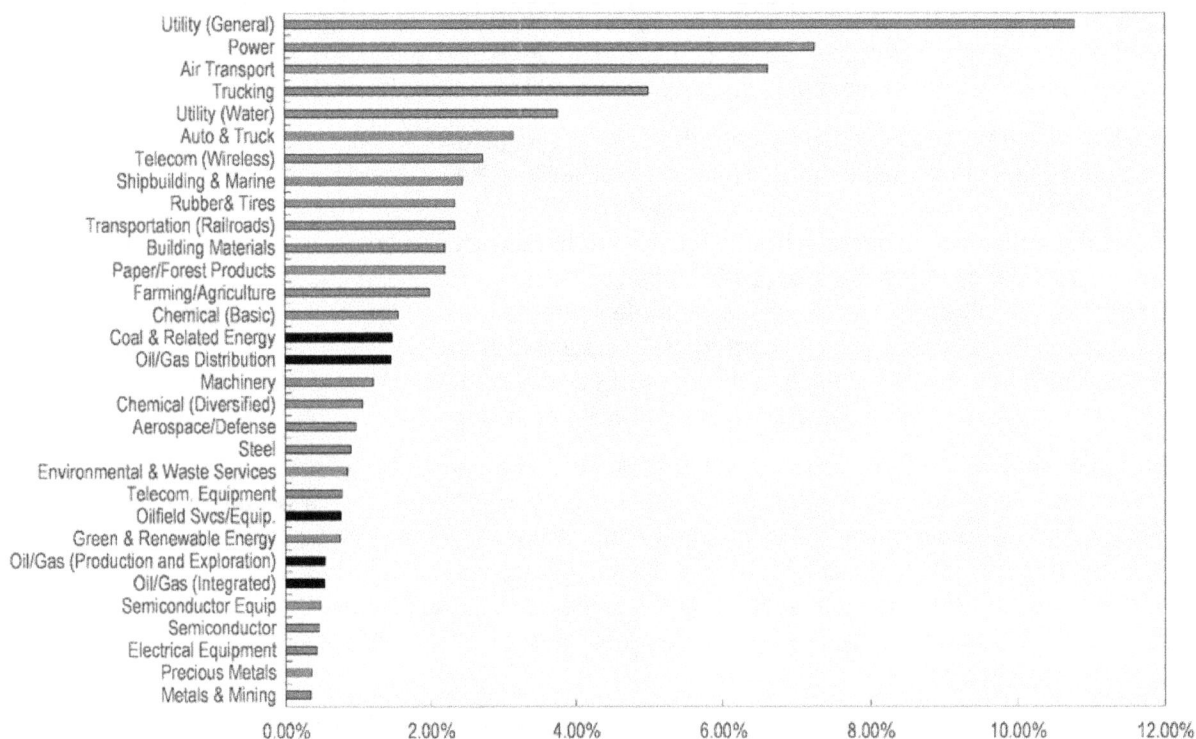

Note: The effect of taxation on the sector-level capital cost is calculated as an average across firms in each sector using the average cost of capital for each sector and not the user cost of capital, which would take into account the depreciation rate for assets used in the sector. This measure indicates how taxation influences the cost of raising funds through equity and debt for firms and does not account for the tax incentives nor the depreciation of assets in the sector. Thus, it is a narrower measure. The tax rate used for this calculation is the effective tax rate, defined by the total taxes paid divided by taxable income, and not the marginal tax rate, which would have been the more appropriate tax rate. Firms included in the sample used to calculate industry-wide averages are publicly traded.
Source: Data from Aswath Damodaran (2021), "Cost of capital by industry" (database), pages.stern.nyu.edu/~adamodar/New_Home_Page/datafile/wacc.htm (accessed 15 March 2021).

EMTRs can also be used for cross-country comparison to identify fiscal regimes that favour more than others the expansion of the extractive industry, circumventing some of the challenges associated with cross-country comparisons based on tax expenditure estimates. However, as noted above, EMTRs are limited to marginal investment decisions and are indicators of the scale of an investment; they are not indicators of the impact of taxation on the discrete choice of where to locate a new investment.

Another ETR indicator that can be used to complement the information delivered by a marginal analysis – or as a stand-alone indicator – is the effective average tax rate (EATR). Unlike the EMTR, the EATR is concerned with discrete investment decisions about where to locate project development. It uses cash flow analysis to shed light on whether the tax system encourages new investment to occur in the first place, i.e. at the extensive margin. More specifically, the EATR relies on a project-level internal rate of return, which ensures that the project is viable over the course of its lifespan. It is expressed as a share of the project's economic profits and gives the percentage of economic profit that is taxed away (Dressler, Hanappi and van Dender, 2018[20]).

The EATR indicates how a fiscal regime can facilitate investment in new fossil-fuel projects, but it requires assumptions about the level of profitability that is representative of the industry. Because such assumptions can differ dramatically from one oil field or coal mining project to another, the EMTR, which only requires measuring the user cost of capital, might be less sensitive to such specifications. The EATR, on the other hand, has the potential to better reflect investment decisions in the resource sector because it summarises tax incentives for investments that earn an economic profit, or a return that is greater than the normal return required on a marginal investment.

The OECD uses fiscal models to calculate economic indicators such as EATR and EMTR. Building on OECD efforts in documenting and modelling economy-wide corporate effective tax rates, effective tax rates in the electricity sector and R&D tax subsidies, there is scope to expand these models to account for specificities of fossil-fuel extractive industries.[7] Also, the International Monetary Fund provides an open-source tool, the Fiscal Analysis of Resource Industries (FARI) model, to generate EATR and EMTR as well as other outcomes such as government revenue raised under different fiscal regimes. These OECD and IMF tools remain partial, however, as they take production and investment paths as exogenous parameters.

2.4.2. Other tools available to evaluate distortiveness in the upstream sector

Modelling production of oil and gas, using an optimal extraction model such as the one developed by (Anderson, Kellogg and Salant, 2018[21]), can be highly complementary. Optimal extraction models can provide a more comprehensive evaluation of the distortiveness of different fossil-fuel fiscal regimes as they can quantify production volumes. For example, (Daubanes and Andrade de Sá, 2014[16]) and (Gaudet and Lasserre, 2015[17]) study the impact of different tax provisions on exploration and extraction outcomes, though not quantitatively. (Anderson, Kellogg and Salant, 2018[21]) model the drilling decisions of firms and under simplifying assumptions, as in (Metcalf, 2018[22]), it is possible to analytically derive the additional drilling activity and production induced by preferential tax treatment.

The impact of fiscal regimes on trade can be inferred. For instance (Metcalf, 2018[22]) constructs a simple model of an oil and of a gas market and calibrates it to reproduce a future global oil price provided by different forecast scenarios. The study draws on the literature of supply and demand elasticities to provide a back-of-the-envelope calculation of the impact of tax preferences on macroeconomic outcomes such as global prices, domestic and international supply, and domestic demand. As for the environmental implications of such incentives, the resulting excess production can be converted into CO_2-equivalent quantities and the associated welfare loss can be derived using the social cost of these emissions.

2.4.3. Evaluating distortions from fossil-fuel support for industrial end-user sectors

A focus on firms' decisions in response to government support measures allows analysis of one of the more relevant concerns for OECD and G20 countries over reform of support for fossil fuels: the potentially deleterious consequences of reform on domestic energy-using industries. Tax expenditures on energy used by industries are the main support instrument that directly affects their use of fossil fuels. Economic theory can help guide discussion on how support for fossil fuels causes distortions in the investment, production and consumption decisions of industrial firms.

As with the method proposed for the upstream sector, distortions generated by support measures for fossil-fuel users can be captured by evaluating how fiscal regimes might reduce the user cost of capital in a given sector. An ETR for end-user industries indicates the extent to which support creates incentives for investment in fossil-fuel consuming industries through preferential tax treatment of their energy inputs. Industry-country specific ETRs can also point to industries that benefit the most from government support and thus reveal the potential impacts of reform across sectors. The OECD's *Taxing Energy Use* (TEU) and *Effective Carbon Rates* (ECR) databases provide effective tax rates for energy use, including for industrial users (OECD, 2019[23]; OECD, 2018[24]). Data therein show that 76.5% of emissions are priced below EUR 30/tCO$_2$, with at least 80% of industrial emissions completely unpriced (OECD, 2018[24]).[8] The integration of information on tax expenditures for energy inputs could strengthen the capacity of the TEU and ECR databases to inform on capital-related distortions created by the fiscal regime (Hanappi, 2018[25]).

Another approach to measuring the direct impact of fossil-fuel support on resource allocation for end users is through modelling behavioural responses of end-user industries to government support measures. Given the prevalence among OECD member countries of tax expenditures for energy-intensive industries, a modelling framework similar to that used in (Fullerton and Heutel, 2007[26])and (Heutel and Kelly, 2016[27]) would be suitable to derive and analyse the effect of different types of support measures commonly used to benefit downstream industries. This type of framework provides analytical expressions for the impact of distortionary support measures on output and the allocation of factors of production across two sectors: an energy-intensive sector and a non-energy-intensive one.

The model is in a closed-economy setting but can be extended to take into account trade effects. In the model, the energy-intensive sector is one that uses energy as a factor of production in addition to labour and capital; the second sector employs only non-energy factors of production. The model is flexible enough to evaluate the role of different support mechanisms benefiting end-user industries, a fossil-fuel excise tax reduction being one of them. Additionally, results from such a model enable estimation of the environmental implications of government support through a conversion of energy-use into burnable emissions.

Countries that provide tax expenditures on energy products for their industrial sectors often claim that these measures are necessary to maintain their domestic industries' international competitiveness and prevent relocation of polluting industries to less environmentally stringent countries. Several empirical studies on differential energy price impacts on firms' performance find that this impact is smaller than others.[9] Modelling behavioural responses of end-user industries could complement insights from these empirical studies to further reveal the impact of tax expenditures and other transfers on end-user industries performance.

Another advantage to using the modelling framework proposed in (Fullerton and Heutel, 2007[26]) and (Heutel and Kelly, 2016[27]) is that the functional form of supply and demand equations need not be specified, and the data needed to calculate the impact of tax reductions on production decisions are available. Energy, capital and labour use at the sector level are available for OECD and some partner economies. Factor shares and factor expenditure shares in total sector income can also be measured. Elasticities of substitution between inputs and outputs can be informed by the vast literature dedicated to their estimation.

There are limitations, however, to the use of the proposed modelling framework. Since its equilibrium outcomes are derived from a linearised approximation of the underlying model, it is only considered robust enough for measuring small changes in tax rates, up to 10%. It is also too simple to derive precise point estimates for effects, although it can provide a robust indication of the direction of the impacts.

2.4.4. Evaluating distortions resulting from fossil-fuel support to end-use consumption outside the industrial sector (residential, transportation, commercial)

Underpricing fossil-fuel products relative to market prices or cost recovery by regulating domestic prices or reducing tax rates, and hence end-user prices, increases consumption of fuels relative to an efficient pricing counterpart. (Coady et al., 2017[28]) provide analysis on the fiscal, welfare and environmental distortions caused by underpricing fossil fuels. Their analysis uses a stylised long-run comparative static framework to provide insights on the potential gains from correcting the underpricing of fossil fuels, to reflect the social cost of carbon.[10] Similarly, (Davis, 2014[29]) and (Davis, 2017[30]) measure the effect of underpricing road fuels on consumption and the resulting costs to society, or "deadweight loss", by taking into account the private cost of fossil fuels (as set by international markets or cost recovery), the cost of externalities, end-user prices, and demand and supply elasticities. (Jacobsen et al., 2016[31]) offer another way to measure the deadweight loss of second-best energy policies (i.e. opposed to direct pricing of carbon) for internalising the external costs. Their proposed method demonstrates that regression results of the externality on the policy instrument can have welfare implications provided that certain conditions are met. Rather than relying on demand or supply elasticity estimates, this method requires data on the distribution of the externality (e.g. carbon emissions) and the policy instrument used (e.g. effective energy prices).

2.4.5. Evaluating the incidence of fossil-fuel support

It is not always straightforward to ascertain the incidence of government support measures because those who are directly targeted or eligible for support are not necessarily those who benefit from it; the statutory incidence and the economic incidence of support are not always the same. Fossil-fuel taxes are important fiscal instruments deployed to raise revenues and to internalise negative externalities associated with the use of fossil fuels. The price pass-through of such instruments is highly dependent on the market structure and its price-setting behaviour. When the market is competitive, firms shift the burden of energy taxes completely onto consumers; in imperfectly competitive settings, the pass-through of price changes to consumers can be more or less proportional to the changes in tax rates (Fullerton and Metcalf, 2002[32]) and (Flues and Thomas, 2015[33]).

At the same time, tax expenditures that reduce the prevailing statutory tax rate on energy products for some consumer classes, such as agricultural and manufacturing sectors, are pervasive among OECD and G20 countries. It is important to understand the implications of these tax expenditures for household income and consumption to gauge the extent to which the benefits are passed on to consumers, including across income-levels, and potential equity issues. Micro-simulation models that use household surveys with data on income and expenditure are specifically designed to study such questions.

In emerging and less developed countries, consumer price support is a policy tool that has been used, among other objectives, to extend energy access and affordability as well as alleviate poverty, particularly in resource-rich countries. Several country studies have shown that the underpricing of energy products disproportionally benefits richer households (Arze del Granado, Coady and Gillingham, 2012[34]) and (Lustig et al., 2013[35]). Tools to analyse the distribution of such support across income groups are widely available within the OECD and externally; Commitment to Equity (CEQ) Institute and the IMF, among other entities, have built publicly accessible toolkits to this end.

2.4.6. Prioritising fossil-fuel support measures for reform

This last step towards assessing the distortiveness of support measures for fossil fuels is to develop indicators on different outcomes – ETRs, production, investment, consumption, environmental and welfare – that capture the impact of one measure versus another. The analytical tools discussed above indicate that a cost-effective way to ascertain distortions is to measure the support measures against the reference fiscal regime. The ratios between the reference case and the case with a given support policy can be used to rank support measures along different dimensions.

In the case of ETR analysis, the difference between the ETRs delivered through a chosen reference fiscal regime can be used as the baseline to gauge the effects of different tax provisions on the allocation of capital across sectors. The EMTR differential between the oil and gas sector and the reference fiscal system, for example, reveals the relative treatment of the concerned industries and thus the relative incentives offered for incremental investments. Differences in EATRs between the reference case and the tax regime that includes a support measure would indicate the relative incentives delivered to new investments (i.e. at the extensive margin). Investment distortions can be analysed with reference to several dimensions: timing, asset types, jurisdictions, and sectors (Mckenzie, 2016[36]). The effective tax analysis, while comprehensive in terms of the tax provisions it can assess, stops short of delivering insights on the relative impact of different support measures on other behavioural outcomes of interest.

Partial equilibrium models by (Anderson, Kellogg and Salant, 2018[21]) and general equilibrium models by (Heutel and Kelly, 2016[27]) are examples of analytical frameworks that can shed light on how different support policies deliver different production, investment and consumption outcomes, and environmental and welfare implications compared with a reference fiscal regime. Eventually, the different policies can be ranked according to their impact along these different dimensions. Policies that create the largest deviations from a reference fiscal regime could be put forward for reform.

2.5. Identifying and quantifying adverse effects that might hinder reform

The analytical frameworks described above are useful for identifying the most distortive measures that can be considered good candidates for reform. However, they provide a limited assessment of the consequences of reform. By not taking into account the forward and backward linkages between upstream fossil-fuel producers and downstream industrial consumers and other end users (e.g. transport and residential users), they reveal little about the implications of reforms.

The phasing out of fossil-fuel support may have some unwanted economic and social effects that could hamper the political acceptance of reform and jeopardise reform processes. These possible effects should be anticipated by assessing the distributional consequences of reform and likely implications for the performance of firms and industries of increasing energy and capital costs. The analytical tools discussed in this section can shed light on possible impacts of reforms and help identify potential winners and losers.

Adverse effects of reforming fossil-fuel support can be direct or indirect. Direct effects result from behavioural responses of individuals and firms targeted by the specific government support. Indirect effects result from price changes for inputs and outputs throughout the fossil-fuel value chain that shift consumption and production patterns and can induce macroeconomic and trade effects. Two approaches are widely used to evaluate the impacts of reforms: empirical and modelling-based methods.

2.5.1. Econometric studies using micro-data

Econometric studies that examine distributional consequences of policies provide precise information on the effect of reform on consumption demand – or more generally their welfare implications – by studying the erosion of household income or firm competitiveness. They often rely on surveys with highly detailed data, at the firm or the household level, on expenditures and incomes. Econometric studies using household or firm surveys can provide important information on the groups affected by the phasing out of fossil-fuel support and the magnitude of this impact. The micro-data provided by the survey allows for precise assessment of distributional effects of reforms, including effects on poverty or inequality. Survey-based tools may also prove useful to simulate alternative compensation measures accompanying reform (an increase of means-tested benefits, for instance).

The OECD has used household budget surveys to investigate effects of energy tax reform across different income and demographic groups (Flues and Thomas, 2015[33]). Other institutions have also developed open-source modules to help policy makers understand the distributional impacts of reforms based on household surveys. The IMF developed a tool for analysing the distributional impacts of fuel subsidy reforms emanating from both direct and indirect effects of price changes on household income (Fabrizio, Goumilevski and Kpodar, 2016[37]). The Commitment to Equity (CEQ) Institute developed a framework to analyse the incidence of taxes and benefits and applied it to a range of low- to medium-income countries (e.g. (Enami and Lustig, 2018[38])).[11]

However, survey-based studies suffer from limitations. Their coverage is restricted to a country, region or sector, which weakens the general validity of their conclusions. They cannot account for spillover effects that fall outside the scope of the analysis and may not allow for dynamic responses to an initial policy change, as they often provide only short-term information on the incidence of reforms and do not capture behavioural responses.

2.5.2. Structural and computable general equilibrium models

Structural models provide additional insight into the possible impacts of reforms since their outputs are more complete and they can enable dynamic and long-term predictions of responses to initial policy shocks. These models, which posit a partial assessment (sectoral) or a general equilibrium assessment (at the country or global level), simulate the reform considering a set of equations defining the relationships between economic agents, and compare the results thus obtained to a business-as-usual scenario. Sectoral models are useful to precisely assess impacts for the energy sector or other specific industries, though computable general equilibrium (CGE) models are usually favoured at the country or global level, as they provide more complete information on macroeconomic variables and greenhouse gas emissions. CGE models can be dynamic and introduce markets' responses to a policy reform and transition, and structural changes for the medium and long term. They are also modular and can be extended to account for more indirect and feedback effects of households on upstream sectors.

The OECD uses CGE models tailored to specific policy areas that can be used to study potential adverse impacts of fossil-fuel support reform processes. The OECD ENV-Linkages CGE model is used to study climate change mitigation policy; the OECD Trade model METRO (ModElling TRade at the OECD) has been developed to explore the economic impact of changes on policy, technology and other factors. The ENV-Linkages model was used to examine the macroeconomic, environmental and distribution consequences of energy subsidy reforms applied to Indonesia (Durand-Lasserve et al., 2015[39]). The model was extended to account for households' income distribution since its generic form limits the analysis to a single representative household type. By accommodating household heterogeneity, the CGE model delivers insights on how the effects are felt by different groups in the population. In the same vein, the METRO model is undergoing an extension to accommodate distributional effects by mapping the information from household budget surveys to the model's structure (OECD, 2021[40]).

Several universities and research institutions have energy-specific models, such as the University College London Energy Institute's suite of energy models, ranging from a bottom-up model, BUEGO, which captures project-level oil and gas extraction information, to an integrated assessment model, TIAM-UCL-IAM, which aims to capture the complexity of the climate system (UCL, 2021[41]).

The main modelling tools used to evaluate the effects of reforming fossil-fuel support can provide much information (Table 2.2). They still have shortcomings, however. They are data and resource-intensive and often rely on fixed parameters (for instance, the proportion of income saved by households), which may change over time. These parameters are often determined by empirical studies, the results of which may be hard to extrapolate. Computing capabilities also limit the extent to which particular industries and countries (or regions) can be singled out, thus narrowing the range of questions that models can address.

As a consequence, structural models should not be considered as precisely predictive, but as a tool to anticipate likely effects. They can also be complemented with insights from survey-based analysis.

Table 2.2. Modelling tools for studying the impact of reform of fossil-fuel support

Scope	Indicators	Tools
Macroeconomy	Gross domestic product Inflation Public debt Employment	Computable general equilibrium model
Firms	Competitiveness Redistribution between firms or sectors	Micro-simulations based on firm surveys Empirical model Sectoral model Computable general equilibrium model (with specific add-on)
Households	Inequality Poverty Redistribution across income groups	Micro-simulations based on household surveys Computable general equilibrium model (with social add-on)
Environment	Greenhouse gas emissions	Computable general equilibrium model Micro-simulation models based on household and firm surveys

2.6. Finding alternatives to subsidised activities

Since fossil-fuel support programmes are diffused throughout the economy, affecting economic, social and environmental outcomes, their reform should be accompanied by alternative measures that not only alleviate any negative effects of reforms, but also channel the resulting fiscal savings to more productive uses. In that sense, an inclusive fossil-fuel support reform necessitates a whole-economy approach and should be pursued as part of broader energy transition agendas that have at their heart the aim of protecting vulnerable populations from harm.

Given the diversity of countries providing support for fossil fuels, country-specific reform packages, including alternative policy measures, should be designed to ensure a low-emissions energy transition that enables economic growth and social inclusion. Fossil-fuel capital assets and reserves run the highest risk of becoming stranded as governments put mitigating and adapting to climate change at the forefront of their policy agendas. Transition programmes for concerned sectors, as in the case of coal, should be anticipated, especially as pressure mounts for countries to phase out coal-fired power plants.

An organising concept used in economics to evaluate alternative policy options is the criterion of Pareto or near-Pareto improvements, whereby policy reform increases welfare compared with a situation without reform. Despite the considerable scope for reducing distortions from fossil-fuel support, there can be trade-offs between economically efficient policies, "equitable" income distribution and better environmental outcomes. When existing policies are poorly designed, their reform can worsen both efficiency and distributional outcomes. In other cases, the prospect of reform can pose difficult political choices. Therefore, designing alternative policies requires a balancing act among these different goals. Clearly stated policy objectives, which harness synergies among seemingly disparate policy areas, can facilitate designing a Pareto-improving reform agenda.

Insights from empirical and simulation work into the distributional effects of reforms across households and firms will help identify the groups that would be most affected by reform and alternative strategies to alleviate adverse effects. OECD work and the broader literature have shown that economic and distributional improvements, as well as emissions reductions, tend to result from better-targeted fuel subsidies or means-tested cash transfers rather than from broader consumer price support, i.e.

government regulation that lowers domestic prices relative to market prices. The OECD's Going for Growth work stream, which looks at structural reforms in policy areas identified as priorities to boost income, inclusiveness and sustainability in OECD and selected partner economies, identifies reform priorities for each country addressed. It does so in an integrated way, so as to provide reform packages that account for the synergies and trade-offs among policies to mitigate adverse effects (OECD, 2019[42]). For example, in the case of reforming fossil-fuel support, a combination of increasing energy taxes on firms and lowering labour costs has been identified as an alternative measure to reduce the "deadweight loss" from support, while mitigating the impact of higher energy-input costs. For countries and regions dependent on the revenues from fossil-fuel resources, opportunities for economic development outside the sector should be part and parcel of a reform programme, particularly as unsubsidised coal becomes an unviable source of energy (Morris, Kaufman and Doshi, 2019[43]).

2.7. Conclusions

Reform of support for fossil fuels is often identified as a priority for a country's fiscal consolidation efforts and for climate action to align financial flows with low-carbon pathways. Implementation remains elusive for many countries, however, as they face seemingly irreconcilable policy agendas of economic growth and sustainability, coupled with potential political backlash against austerity and rising costs. The COVID-19 crisis and resulting recession present an opportunity to reform support for fossil fuels as part of efforts to alleviate mounting fiscal pressure and achieve a more efficient and sustainable path as part of economic recovery packages.

The sequential approach set out in this chapter provides analytical tools to underpin a well-informed reform process, including as part of COVID-19 recovery packages, drawing on the OECD's longstanding experience in measuring support measures for fossil fuels. The Inventory sheds light on over 1 300 support measures for fossil fuels, often rooted in complex fiscal legislation. Deploying the tools highlighted in this chapter can help policy makers identify the most distorting government support measures and alternative or complementary policies that deliver desired objectives more efficiently and effectively. The OECD Secretariat stands ready to support countries interested in applying the sequential approach to obtain evidence-based recommendations for reform. In addition, the chapter has highlighted a number of information and analytical gaps along the different steps for reform, suggesting several areas for further work, including analysing effective tax rates and measuring the relative distortiveness of support measures.

References

Anderson, S., R. Kellogg and S. Salant (2018), "Hotelling under Pressure", *Journal of Political Economy*, Vol. 126/3, pp. 984-1026, http://dx.doi.org/10.1086/697203. [21]

Arze del Granado, F., D. Coady and R. Gillingham (2012), "The Unequal Benefits of Fuel Subsidies: A Review of Evidence for Developing Countries", *World Development*, Vol. 40/11, pp. 2234-2248, http://dx.doi.org/10.1016/J.WORLDDEV.2012.05.005. [34]

Coady, D. et al. (2017), "How Large Are Global Fossil Fuel Subsidies?", *World Development*, http://dx.doi.org/10.1016/j.worlddev.2016.10.004. [28]

Conrad, R., B. Hool and D. Nekipelov (2018), "The Role of Royalties in Resource Extraction Contracts", *Land Economics*, Vol. 94/3, pp. 340-353, http://le.uwpress.org/content/94/3/340.full.pdf (accessed on 3 July 2018). [18]

Daubanes, J. and S. Andrade de Sá (2014), "Taxing the Rent of Non-Renewable Resource Sectors: A Theoretical Note", *OECD Economics Department Working Papers*, No. 1149, OECD Publishing, Paris, https://dx.doi.org/10.1787/5jz0zb620vr1-en. [16]

Davis, L. (2017), "The Environmental Cost of Global Fuel Subsidies", *The Energy Journal*, Vol. Volume 38/KAPSARC Special Issue. [30]

Davis, L. (2014), *The economic cost of global fuel subsidies*, American Economic Association, http://dx.doi.org/10.1257/aer.104.5.581. [29]

Dechezleprêtre, A., D. Nachtigall and F. Venmans (2018), "The joint impact of the European Union emissions trading system on carbon emissions and economic performance", *OECD Economics Department Working Papers*, No. 1515, OECD Publishing, Paris, https://dx.doi.org/10.1787/4819b016-en. [48]

Dressler, L., T. Hanappi and K. van Dender (2018), "Unintended technology-bias in corporate income taxation: The case of electricity generation in the low-carbon transition", *OECD Taxation Working Papers*, No. 37, OECD Publishing, Paris, https://dx.doi.org/10.1787/9f4a34ff-en. [20]

Durand-Lasserve, O. et al. (2015), "Modelling of distributional impacts of energy subsidy reforms: an illustration with Indonesia", *OECD Environment Working Papers*, No. 86, OECD Publishing, Paris, https://dx.doi.org/10.1787/5js4k0scrqq5-en. [39]

Elgouacem, A. (2020), "Designing fossil fuel subsidy reforms in OECD and G20 countries: A robust sequential approach methodology", *OECD Environment Working Papers*, No. 168, OECD Publishing, Paris, https://dx.doi.org/10.1787/d888f461-en. [49]

Elgouacem, A. et al. (2020), "The fiscal implications of the low-carbon transition", *OECD Green Growth Papers*, No. 2020/01, OECD Publishing, Paris, https://dx.doi.org/10.1787/6cea13aa-en. [15]

Elgouacem, A. and P. Journeay-Kaler (2020), *The Netherlands's Effort to Phase Out and Rationalise its Fossil-Fuel Subsidies*, OECD/IEA, http://www.oecd.org/fossil-fuels/publication/2020-OECD-IEA-review-of-fossil-fuel-subsidies-in-the-Netherlands.pdf (accessed on 14 January 2021). [6]

Enami, A. and N. Lustig (2018), "Inflation and the Erosion of the Poverty Reduction Impact of Iran's Universal Cash Transfer", *Commitment to Equity (CEQ) Working Paper Series*, https://ideas.repec.org/p/tul/ceqwps/68.html#download (accessed on 17 September 2018). [38]

Fabrizio, S., A. Goumilevski and K. Kpodar (2016), *A New Tool for Distributional Incidence Analysis: An Application to Fuel Subsidy Reform*, IMF, https://www.imf.org/external/pubs/ft/tnm/2016/tnm1607.pdf (accessed on 17 September 2018). [37]

Faehn, T. et al. (2017), "Climate Policies in a Fossil Fuel Producing Country: Demand versus Supply Side Policies", *The Energy Journal*, Vol. 38/1, http://dx.doi.org/10.5547/01956574.38.1.tfae. [13]

Flues, F. and B. Lutz (2015), "Competitiveness Impacts of the German Electricity Tax", *OECD Environment Working Papers*, No. 88, OECD Publishing, Paris, https://dx.doi.org/10.1787/5js0752mkzmv-en. [46]

Flues, F. and A. Thomas (2015), "The distributional effects of energy taxes", *OECD Taxation Working Papers*, No. 23, OECD Publishing, Paris, https://dx.doi.org/10.1787/5js1qwkqqrbv-en. [33]

Fullerton, D. and G. Heutel (2007), "The general equilibrium incidence of environmental taxes ☆", *Journal of Public Economics*, Vol. 91, pp. 571-591, http://dx.doi.org/10.1016/j.jpubeco.2006.07.004. [26]

Fullerton, D. and G. Metcalf (2002), "Chapter 26 Tax incidence", *Handbook of Public Economics*, Vol. 4, pp. 1787-1872, http://dx.doi.org/10.1016/S1573-4420(02)80005-2. [32]

Garsous, G. and T. Kozluk (2017), "Foreign Direct Investment and The Pollution Haven Hypothesis: Evidence from Listed Firms", *OECD Economics Department Working Papers*, No. 1379, OECD Publishing, Paris, https://dx.doi.org/10.1787/1e8c0031-en. [47]

Gaudet, G. and P. Lasserre (2015), *The taxation of nonrenewable natural resources*, https://www.cirano.qc.ca/files/publications/2015s-19.pdf (accessed on 11 September 2018). [17]

Green, F. and R. Denniss (2018), "Cutting with both arms of the scissors: the economic and political case for restrictive supply-side climate policies", *Climatic Change*, Vol. 150/1-2, pp. 73-87, http://dx.doi.org/10.1007/s10584-018-2162-x. [11]

Hanappi, T. (2018), "Corporate Effective Tax Rates: Model Description and Results from 36 OECD and Non-OECD Countries", *OECD Taxation Working Papers*, No. 38, OECD Publishing, Paris, https://dx.doi.org/10.1787/a07f9958-en. [25]

Herr, M. (2020), "A Global Registry of Fossil Fuels is Needed to Hold Governments and Corporations Accountable for Emissions from Current and Planned Production", *The Fossil Fuel Non-Proliferation Treaty Initiative*, https://static1.squarespace.com/static/5dd3cc5b7fd99372fbb04561/t/5f5a8b6012ada617bd335b5b/1599769442593/Global+Registry+of+Fossil+Fuels+Press+Release.pdf (accessed on 14 January 2021). [14]

Heutel, G. and D. Kelly (2016), "Incidence, Environmental, and Welfare Effects of Distortionary Subsidies", *Journal of the Association of Environmental and Resource Economists*, Vol. 3/2, pp. 361-415, http://dx.doi.org/10.1086/684578. [27]

Jacobsen, M. et al. (2016), "Sufficient Statistics for Imperfect Externality-Correcting Policies", http://www.nber.org/papers/w22063 (accessed on 2 November 2018). [31]

Jésus, F. et al. (2017), *Towards a G7 target to phase out environmentally harmful subsidies*, OECD, Paris, https://www.minambiente.it/sites/default/files/archivio/allegati/sviluppo_sostenibile/background_paper_4_G7_env_OECD_Towards_G7_target_to_phase_out_EHSs.pdf (accessed on 14 January 2021). [3]

Lustig, N. et al. (2013), "The impact of taxes and social spending on inequality and poverty in Argentina, Bolivia, Brazil, Mexico, Peru and Uruguay: an overview", Commitment to Equity (CEQ) Institute, http://www.commitmentoequity.org. (accessed on 18 September 2018). [35]

Mckenzie, K. (2016), "Inside the back box: marginal effect tax rates on capital in canada - primer", pp. 795-816. [36]

McKenzie, K. and J. Mintz (2011), "The Tricky Art of Measuring Fossil Fuel Subsidies: A Critique of Existing Studies", *The School of Public Policy Publications*, Vol. 4/0, http://dx.doi.org/10.11575/SPPP.V4I0.42638. [19]

Metcalf, G. (2018), "The Impact of Removing Tax Preferences for US Oil and Natural Gas Production: Measuring Tax Subsidies by an Equivalent Price Impact Approach", *Journal of the Association of Environmental and Resource Economists*, Vol. 5/1, pp. 1-37, http://dx.doi.org/10.1086/693367. [22]

Morris, A., N. Kaufman and S. Doshi (2019), *The risk of fiscal collapse in coal-reliant communities*, Columbia University and Brooking, https://www.brookings.edu/wp-content/uploads/2019/07/RiskofFiscalCollapseinCoalReliantCommunities-CGEP_Report_080619.pdf (accessed on 30 August 2019). [43]

OECD (2021), *METRO trade model: The OECD's tool for analysing global markets*, OECD, https://www.oecd.org/trade/topics/metro-trade-model/ (accessed on 14 January 2021). [40]

OECD (2021), *OECD Environmental Performance Reviews: Ireland 2021 (forthcoming)*. [4]

OECD (2021), *OECD.Stat: Query Wizard for International Development Statistics*, OECD, https://stats.oecd.org/qwids/ (accessed on 14 January 2021). [9]

OECD (2019), *Budgeting and Public Expenditures in OECD Countries 2019*, OECD Publishing, Paris, https://dx.doi.org/10.1787/9789264307957-en. [5]

OECD (2019), *Economic Policy Reforms 2019: Going for Growth*, OECD Publishing, Paris, https://dx.doi.org/10.1787/aec5b059-en. [42]

OECD (2019), "Measuring distortions in international markets: the aluminium value chain", *OECD Trade Policy Papers*, No. 218, OECD Publishing, Paris, https://dx.doi.org/10.1787/c82911ab-en. [45]

OECD (2019), *Taxing Energy Use 2019: Using Taxes for Climate Action*, OECD Publishing, Paris, https://dx.doi.org/10.1787/058ca239-en. [23]

OECD (2018), *Effective Carbon Rates 2018: Pricing Carbon Emissions Through Taxes and Emissions Trading*, OECD Publishing, Paris, https://dx.doi.org/10.1787/9789264305304-en. [24]

OECD (2018), *OECD Companion to the Inventory of Support Measures for Fossil Fuels 2018*, OECD Publishing, Paris, https://dx.doi.org/10.1787/9789264286061-en. [10]

OECD (2015), *OECD Companion to the Inventory of Support Measures for Fossil Fuels 2015*, OECD Publishing, Paris, https://dx.doi.org/10.1787/9789264239616-en. [44]

OECD (2015), *OECD Companion to the Inventory of Support Measures for Fossil Fuels 2015*, OECD Publishing, Paris, http://dx.doi.org/10.1787/9789264239616-en. [7]

OECD (2007), *Subsidy Reform and Sustainable Development: Political Economy Aspects*, OECD Sustainable Development Studies, OECD Publishing, Paris, https://dx.doi.org/10.1787/9789264019379-en. [2]

OECD (2005), *Environmentally Harmful Subsidies: Challenges for Reform*, OECD Publishing, Paris, https://dx.doi.org/10.1787/9789264012059-en. [1]

Piggot, G. et al. (2018), "Swimming upstream: addressing fossil fuel supply under the UNFCCC", *Climate Policy*, Vol. 18/9, pp. 1189-1202, http://dx.doi.org/10.1080/14693062.2018.1494535. [12]

UCL (2021), *Energy models at the UCL Energy Institute*, University College London, https://www.ucl.ac.uk/energy-models/ (accessed on 14 January 2021). [41]

UN Environment, OECD and IISD (2019), *Measuring fossil fuel subsidies in the context of the sustainable development goals*, UN Environment, Nairobi, Kenya, https://wedocs.unep.org/bitstream/handle/20.500.11822/28111/FossilFuel.pdf?sequence=1&isAllowed=y (accessed on 23 September 2019). [8]

Notes

[1] This chapter is adapted from a 2020 OECD Environment Working Paper by Assia Elgouacem. For further detail and technical discussion, see (Elgouacem, 2020[49]). The chapter focuses on G20 and OECD member countries, consistent with the bulk of the countries reflected in the OECD Inventory.

[2] A comprehensive discussion of the taxonomy of support measures can be found in Chapter 2 of the *OECD Companion to the Inventory of Support Measures for Fossil Fuels 2015* (OECD, 2015[44]).

[3] Formal incidence (*de jure* incidence) is to be distinguished from economic incidence, which takes into account supply and demand elasticities and looks at *de facto* final beneficiaries of a measure, and is therefore much more difficult to establish. The OECD Inventory approach builds on the OECD's PSE-CSE accounting framework for measuring support to particular industries, used to measure support for the agriculture sector since the mid-1980s and the fisheries sector since the late 1990s.

[4] Depending on how transparent or systematic a country is in its budgetary reporting processes, many if not most induced transfers will be captured in direct budgetary transfer reporting.

[5] See, for example, OECD work on aluminium sector subsidies (OECD, 2019[45]).

[6] In addition, the combined OECD-IEA estimates do not include producer support estimates for largest fossil-fuel exporting developing countries, because the IEA price gap methodology that covers these countries does not pick up policies that support fossil-fuel production but do not directly impact on end-user prices. Further, governments are funnelling major additional resources to fossil-fuel industries as part of COVID-19 recovery packages, with preliminary estimates in the order of at least USD 235 billion.

[7] (Hanappi, 2018[25]), (Dressler, Hanappi and van Dender, 2018[20]).

[8] The EUR 30/tCO$_2$ benchmark represents a conservative estimate of the social cost of carbon.

[9] (Flues and Lutz, 2015[46]), (Garsous and Kozluk, 2017[47]), and (Dechezleprêtre, Nachtigall and Venmans, 2018[48]) are among studies tackling the issue of competitiveness and carbon leakage.

[10] For the IMF, under-pricing of fossil fuels is measured relative to an efficient price level that comprises environmental and health externalities.

[11] These tools have been mostly used to study the impacts of fuel price reforms on household incomes in developing countries.

Annex A. Methodological approach to tracking aspects of fossil fuel support

Isolating the output-based support to the electricity sector attributable to fossil fuels

The range of fuels and energy products in broad categories covered by the Inventory are coal, natural gas, petroleum products and end-use electricity. There are cases where some measures in the Inventory benefit more than one type of fossil fuels. In this case, the OECD Secretariat allocated support to particular fuels where official government sources do not provide such a breakdown. Measures benefiting more than one fuel or energy product were allocated according to the relative value of production or consumption using the calculated shares derived from the national balances published in the IEA's World Energy Balances.

For fuels such as coal, natural gas and petroleum, the allocation concludes with a simple allocation of shares calculated using the IEA World Energy Balances data. However, for end-use electricity, the allocation presents an additional methodological challenge as raw amounts include embedded support for electricity generated from non-fossil-fuel origin (e.g., nuclear, renewables, biofuels and wastes) and electricity from traded (i.e., imported) sources, (which can make it difficult to trace the ultimate origin and consequently the generation type of the electricity once joining the national grid). Both the share of electricity from non-fossil-fuel sources and electricity from traded sources must therefore be removed to isolate end-use electricity support to fossil fuels alone.

To isolate the share of electricity domestically generated in the country (i.e., excluding imported electricity), the following formula was used:

$$
Ind\_gen_x = \begin{cases} (PowerPl\_gen - TES\_elec)/PowerPl\_gen, & \text{if } PowerPl\_gen >= TES\_elec \\ 1, & \text{if } TES < 0 \text{ (i.e., country is net electricity exporter)} \\ 0, & \text{if } PowerPl\_gen - TES\_elec < 0 \text{ (i.e., country is net electricity importer)} \end{cases}
$$

where:

$PowerPl\_gen = Main\_elec\_gen + Auto\_elec\_gen + Main\_CHP\_gen + Auto\_CHP\_gen$

Ind_gen_x - indigenous electricity generation for country x

TES_elec – total energy supply under electricity for country x

To isolate fossil-fuel from non-fossil-fuel generated electricity, shares from national electricity generation mix from the IEA Energy Balances were used. The following formula was used to calculate the share of fossil-fuel electricity generated per economy:

$$FF\_share_x = (Total\_gen - REN\_gen - Nuclear\_gen)/Total\_gen$$

where:

FF_share_x – share of fossil fuel generated electricity in country x

$Total\_gen$ – total electricity generated by power plants in country x

Ren_gen - total electricity generated by renewable power plants in country x.

- consists of the sum of electricity generation from HYDRO, GEOTHERM, SOLARPV, SOLARTH, TIDE, WIND, MUNWASTER, PRIMSBIO, BIOGASES, BIOGASOL, BIODIESEL, OBIOLIQ, RENEWNS and CHARCOAL from the IEA World Energy Balances (IEA, 2020[1]).

$Nuclear\_gen$ – total electricity generated by nuclear power plants in country x

After obtaining these two coefficients for each country, the share of support attributable to end-use fossil-fuel electricity for a given measure y is then calculated as follows:

$$End\text{-}use\ electricity\ support\ from\ fossil\ fuels = (raw\ amounts\ for\ measure\ y) *(Ind\_gen)* (FF\_share)$$

In summary, the above formula only attributes a certain support amount to end-use electricity support using the share of electricity indigenously generated in the country and the share of electricity generation mix from fossil fuels. In particular, the above formula removes shares that are due to electricity imports (whose ultimate generation origin cannot be determined with the available information) as well as non-fossil-fuel generation sources.

Breaking down fossil-fuel support data to economic sector beneficiaries

Prior to the pilot sectoral disaggregation, the Inventory was organised following the OECD's PSE-CSE framework. Under this classification framework, measures benefitting fossil-fuel producers are classified under Producer Support Estimate (PSE) while those that benefit individual fossil-fuel consumers fall under the Consumer Support Estimate (CSE). A third category, the General Services Support Estimate (GSSE) is assigned for measures that do not increase production or consumption of fossil fuels at present but may do so in the future.

Classification under the PSE-CSE classification framework is broad and does not allow further disaggregation of beneficiaries by economic sector. While it allows to isolate which measures benefit the upstream or midstream fossil-fuel sectors, it does not allow to isolate and pinpoint in greater detail the final end-user economic sectors (e.g. industrial, transport, residential, commercial etc.) targeted by fossil-fuel measures. Identifying and quantifying the benefit received by each economic sector in fossil-fuel support is key in order to evaluate the distributional impacts of proposed fossil-fuel reforms as well as in evaluating whether a particular targeted support programme is efficient in reaching their intended beneficiaries.

Sector tagging mechanics for fossil-fuel support measures

For each measure in the Inventory, two types of information are provided: (i) fiscal information on the budgetary transfers or tax expenditures (monetary value) and (ii) textual metadata with contents on a measure's beneficiaries; eligibility criteria; historical background; and any relevant details on data procurement and data processing.

The information on the textual metadata is used to identify which economic sector is benefitted from each measure. In tagging each measure, the economic activity nomenclature follows the classification used in the IEA World Energy Balances flows. Measures can receive a single (in case only one economic sector is benefitted) or multiple sector tags. In case of a single sector tag, the attribution of values is straightforward and all the measure's amounts get assigned to the single sector. However, there are cases where a measure is designed to benefit multiple sectors (e.g., preferential tax rates for natural gas targeting both residential and commercial sectors or some measures targeting both agricultural and road sector fuels). In this case, the amounts that each sector gets allocated is based on the calculated proportions as obtained from the energy consumption figures reported in the IEA World Energy Balances.

Finally, after the sector tagging exercise, the results are aggregated and mapped according to the following broad sectoral categories:

Annex Table A.1. Selected sector dimension tags to identify ocean-related FFS measures

Broad Sector	Remarks and Included Sectors (IEA short names)
Fossil-fuel production	This category comprises measures that benefits the upstream and midstream segment of fossil-fuel production. It includes measures targeted towards the exploration, production, trade (import or export), transportation or storage of fossil fuels. INDPROD, IMPORTS, EXPORTS, STOCKCHA or TPES (if no detail available).
Electricity generation	This category represents measures that provide support to fossil fuels used as inputs in power generation. Only input fuels fall under this category and does not include support for the consumption of generated electricity by end-use consumers. MAINELEC, AUTOELEC, MAINCHP, AUTOCHP, .MAINHEAT, AUTOHEAT
Transport	Measures benefitted under this category includes fuels used in the following transport activities: road vehicles, agricultural and industrial highway use, aircraft for domestic aviation, rail traffic including urban or suburban transport systems, energy used for pipelines transporting fossil-fuels, domestic maritime navigation (i.e., port of departure and arrival of the same country), and all transport not elsewhere specified. DOMESAIR, ROAD, RAIL, PIPELINE, DOMESNAV, TRNONSPE
Residential	Includes consumption by households (including households with employed persons), with fuels used for transport excepted.
Other sectors	Other sectors include measures that support the use of fossil fuels in energy transformation other than electricity and heat generation, industrial and manufacturing, commercial and public services, agriculture, forestry and fisheries and non-energy use. THEAT, TBOILER, TELE, TBLASTFUR, TGASWKS, TCOKEOVS, TPATFUEL, TBKB, TREFINER, TPETCHEM, LIQUEFAC, TNONSPEC, OWNUSE, EMINES, EOILGASEX, EBLASTFUR, EGASWKS, EBIOGAS, ECOKEOVS, EPATFUEL, EBKB, EREFINER, ECOALLIQ, ELNG, EGTL, EPOWERPLT, EPUMPST, ENUC, ECHARCOAL, ENONSPEC, TRANSFER IRONSTL, CHEMICAL, NONMET, PAPERPRO, NONFERR, TEXTILES, MINING, TRANSEQ, MACHINE, FOODPRO, PAPERPRO, WOODPRO, CONSTRUC, INONSPEC RESIDENT, AGRICULT, FISHING, COMMPUB, ONONSPEC, NONENUSE

Source: Adapted from IEA World Energy Balances, (IEA, 2020[1]).

The routines were implemented using Stata to automate the allocation of each measure. At the end of the tagging exercise, each measure is now classified according to three dimensions: (a) fuel(s) benefitted; (b) PSE-CSE indicator and (c) sectoral beneficiaries. For the sectoral aggregates, allocation involved dual dimensions (i.e. fuel and sector), with more than 100 fuel-sector combinations. This made the calculation to be computationally-intensive, with the dual dimension structure requiring $O(n^2)$ polynomial time complexity during the algorithm's execution.

Identifying ocean-related government support for fossil fuels

The OECD Inventory of Fossil-fuel Support Measures is an online database that identifies, documents and estimates direct budgetary support and tax expenditures supporting the production or consumption of fossil fuels (http://www.oecd.org/fossil-fuels/data). The Inventory currently covers 37 OECD member countries, eight non-OECD G20 economies (Brazil, Colombia, the People's Republic of China, India, Indonesia, the Russian Federation, and South Africa) and six EU Eastern Partnership countries (Armenia, Azerbaijan, Belarus, Georgia, Republic of Moldova and Ukraine) and has compiled more than 1 300 individual support measures (both active and terminated ones). In addition to national measures, sub-national support measures for selected economies are also covered (i.e., Australia, Canada, China, Germany and the US).

For each measure, two types of information are provided: (i) fiscal information on the budgetary transfers or tax expenditures (monetary value) and (ii) textual metadata about a measure's beneficiaries, eligibility criteria, historical background, and any relevant information on data procurement and processing.

Following the OECD's PSE-CSE framework, the measures benefitting fossil-fuel producers are classified as the producer support estimate (PSE) while those that benefit individual fossil-fuel consumers are classified under the consumer support estimate (CSE). A third category, the general services support estimate (GSSE), is assigned for measures that do not currently increase fossil-fuel production and consumption but may do so in the future.

The Inventory identifies the type of fossil fuels that benefit from each measure and presents a breakdown of the amount of support by assigning fuel type tags. In cases where this breakdown is not available in official government sources, the OECD performs data transformation procedure to allocate support to individual fuel tags according to the relative value of production or consumption as calculated from the IEA's World Energy Balances database. Note that measures can benefit more than one type of fossil fuel at the same time and can thus receive multiple fuel tags in this respect. For example, a measure granting lower sales tax rates for road transport fuels will receive multiple fuel tags such as motor gasoline, diesel, LPG and natural gas.

Building on this methodology, an additional binary tag is developed for ocean-related government support for fossil fuels.

Search strategy

A search strategy is developed to identify measures directly relating to oceans. First, measures in countries not bounded by a coastline are removed.[1] Second, a keyword search is conducted on both the programme name and description to pre-screen measures and identify potential candidates for ocean-related FFS. The list of keywords includes generic ocean terms, keywords related to off-shore oil and gas, maritime transport, maritime fisheries and the ocean economy more broadly (Annex Table A.2).[2]

Third, additional measures may be identified using the "sector" dimension which labels individual measures following the nomenclature used in the IEA World Energy Balances. Multiple sectors may be assigned to a single measure. Annex Table A.3 lists the sector tags that are used to pre-screen potential candidates for FFS ocean-related policies. Any measure bearing these tags are identified as potentially relating to the ocean.

Finally, following the pre-screening by the automated keyword-based searches, each candidate measure is then individually reviewed in order to eliminate false positives and to ascertain that measures inadvertently flagged as 'negative' have not been omitted.

Annex Table A.2. Keywords used to identify a candidate subset of ocean-related fossil-fuel support measures

ocean, [ ]sea[ ], marine, maritime, offshore, blue, reef, coral, deep-sea, deep-water, sea-bed, benthic, lagoon, mudflat, tidal, mangrove, coast*, coastal, wetland, coastal, marsh salt, marsh, salt-water, brackish
[ ]fish*, aquaculture, mariculture, cod[ ], [ ]tuna, coral*, mussels, oysters, crustacean, mollusc, pelagic, sea-food, aquatic plants
[ ]ship*, shipping, ship-building, boat, vessel, ferry, floating, naval, [ ]port[ ], sea-port, harbour, harbour, dock, sea transport, cargo, ballast, oil spill*, oceanogra*
cruise, tour, touris*, dredg*, sea salt, desali*, hurricane, cyclone, typhoon, flood, biotechnology, robotics, wave, underwater vehicle, continental shelf, EEZ, exclusive economic, arctic, piracy, submarine, undersea, [ ]cable*, seabed, hurricane, cyclone, blue water, cruise, ferry, international water*, [ ]rig[ ], territorial sea, high sea*

Annex Table A.3. Selected sector dimension tags to identify ocean-related fossil-fuel support measures

Sector (IEA shortname)	Remarks
Indigenous production (INDPROD)	This category comprises the production of primary energy such as various types of primary coal and natural gas. Among ocean-related measures falling under this category are measures benefitting oil and natural gas extraction in ***off-shore environments***.
Oil and gas extraction (EOILGASEX)	This category represents the energy which is used for oil and gas extraction. Ocean-related measure under this category are those benefitting ***off-shore oil and gas extraction operations***.
Domestic navigation (DOMESNAV)	Measures benefitted under this category includes fuels delivered to maritime vessels not engaged in domestic l navigation (i.e. determined in terms of the port of departure and port of arrival belonging to the same single country and not by the flag or nationality of the ship). Note that while the voyages considered are domestic, these may involve routes of considerable distance that may transit through foreign countries or international waters.
Fishing (FISHING)	Measures are classified under the fishing sector if the benefitted fuels are used for inland, coastal and deep-sea fishing as well as energy used in the fishing industry. It is recognised that this sector captures fuels used for inland fishing, which is not considered as ocean-related, but this approach is adapted in the absence of more specific breakdown that isolates fuels used for ocean-related purposes under the FISHING sector.

Source: Adapted from IEA (2019), "World energy balances", IEA World Energy Statistics and Balances (database).

Annex Table A.4. Selected examples of ocean-related measures in the fossil-fuel support inventory

Sectors Benefitted	CSE	PSE	GSSE
Indigenous Production		Sales Tax Exemption for Exploration Equipment (Canada)	Norwegian Petroleum Directorate geological surveys (Norway)
Oil and gas extraction	Mineral oil tax exemption for offshore petroleum sector (Norway)	Sales-Tax Exemption for Repairs and Materials Used on Drilling Rigs (United States)	
Domestic navigation	Fuel tax exemption for shipping (Italy)		
Fishing	Fuel tax exemption for fisheries (Korea)		

References

IEA (2020), *World Energy Balances*, International Energy Agency, https://www.iea.org/data-and-statistics?country=WORLD&fuel=Energy%20supply&indicator=TPESbySource (accessed on 14 January 2021). [1]

Notes

[1] Austria, Czech Republic, Hungary, Luxembourg, Slovak Republic and Switzerland.

[2] While entries in the programme name and description fields occasionally appear in their original language, all of these occurrences are consistently translated into English, thus removing the necessity to devise foreign language keywords in the dictionary.